What others are saying about *High Impact Hiring*:

"Please, please, please study this book before you conduct your next selec-tion interview. Postpone it if you must, but don't even attempt to hire an-other employee before you read *High Impact Hiring*. Selection decisions are *the* most important personnel actions any manager takes. If you want to hire the best contributors for your organization, you are personally responsi-ble for being the best interviewer and choice-maker in your organization. *High Impact Hiring* will enable you to fulfill that awesome obligation. Del Still's new book not only offers an immediately useful process, it's chock full of rich case examples and extraordinary practical questions you can use in your very next interview."

Jim Kouzes, co-author
The Leadership Challenge and
Credibility
Chairman and CEO
The Tom Peters Group/Learning Systems

"This book provides advice and practical guidance for anyone who wants to do a better job in building a competent work force. Excellent workers are al-ways in demand. *High Impact Hiring* shows you how to select these talented and highly skilled employees to give your organization a tremendous com-petitive edge."

Barbara Beck
Vice President
Human Resources
Cisco Systems

"The material in this book gives anyone who is involved in the hiring pro-cess a practical system to pick the very best person for the job. It strips away the myths about interviewing and empowers people to become more suc-cessful at building a solid, competent work team."

George W. Scalise
Former Executive Vice President and
Chief Operating Officer
Apple Computer

High Impact Hiring

How to Interview and Select Outstanding Employees

Del J. Still

Second Edition, Revised

Management Development Systems, LLC
Dana Point, CA

High Impact Hiring

How to Interview and Select Outstanding Employees

By Del J. Still

Copyright © 1997, 2001 by Del J. Still

Published by:
Management Development Systems, LLC
32352 Ascension Road, Dana Point, CA 92629
Phone: (949) 661-1669 Fax: (949) 661-9795
Web site: http://www.hireup.com
Email: info@hireup.com

ORDERING INFORMATION
To obtain additional copies, call **(800) 353-1669**, your local bookseller, log on to Amazon.com (http://www.amazon.com), or Barnes & Noble (http://www.Barnesandnoble.com).

ISBN: 0-9654659-8-5
Library of Congress Catalog Card Number: 96-94870

Printed in the United States of America
First Printing 1997
Second Printing 1999
Third Printing (Second Edition) 2001
Fourth Printing (Second Edition) 2002

Dedicated to all of you who are driven to hire outstanding performers and build a winning team.

Table Of Contents

Complete Evaluation Forms and Review Ratings

Should I Pick the Candidate Who is Overqualified?

Complete Background and Reference Checks

Extend the Offer

Bring the New Employee on Board

Here's a True Story.

Build Your Skills Through Practice

Appendix A: Sample Forms

Appendix B: Work Habit Definitions

Appendix C: Sample Interview Questions

Appendix D: Interview Check List

About the Author

Del J. Still has a background in engineering and manufacturing management, as well as in education, training, and organization development. Dr. Still received his Bachelor's degree from the California State University. He earned an MBA at the University of Santa Clara and completed his doctoral work at the University of Southern California. He is in demand as a speaker and presenter for numerous conventions and seminars. He has been quoted in the *Wall Street Journal* and other leading publications.

This book is based on his more than 15 years of research and practical experience in interviewing hundreds of job candidates and training more than 20,000 interviewers in the behavior-based approach to employment interviewing.

Del is also the developer of *Behavior Based Interviewing*. This workshop complements and expands the information in *High Impact Hiring* and sharpens and reinforces the skills needed to conduct interviews and select the right person for the job. *Behavior Based Interviewing* has enabled his clients to save countless thousands of dollars by building a superior workforce and avoiding costly hiring mistakes.

Acknowledgments

It's not possible to cite the scores of people and resources consulted in the writing of this book. My colleagues, friends and family have been extremely supportive and helpful and I would like to express my appreciation to all of you.

A special thanks to my clients. You have taught me so much more about interviewing than my research and experience alone ever could.

My sincere appreciation and gratitude goes out to Rita Risser J.D. at Fair Measures Inc., for her important contributions to the content of Chapter 8 of this book. (http://www.fairmeasures.com)

Rick Dressler, President of Quickshots Inc., is a gifted professional who did a superb job with the design and layout of the book cover.
(http://www.quickshots.com)

My wife Mary played a unique role in the development of *High Impact Hiring*. She constantly supported and encouraged me when times got tough and the end seemed so far away. Like a good shepherd she faithfully pushed, pulled, led, supported, helped, and kept me on the path until the goal was achieved.

Purpose

High Impact Hiring was written to provide information to help you create and conduct high-quality selection interviews. It's not intended to render legal or other professional services. If you need expert advice or assistance, seek the services of a competent expert.

This book will give you a starting point. Learn all you can about interviewing by consulting other sources of information. Then tailor your approach to your specific situation.

Every effort has been made to make this book as complete and accurate as possible. Use the text as a general guide. The author and publisher shall have neither liability nor responsibility for loss or damage caused or alleged to be caused, directly or indirectly by the information contained in *High Impact Hiring*.

Chapter 1

The Road Ahead

Disaster was waiting for me on that warm summer day. I was a young engineering manager. Ron walked into my office for a job interview. It was an internal transfer and I had been warned that Ron couldn't make it in his current job and he was being set up for termination. As I talked with him, I could sense his desperation. Ron was a little older than me, perhaps in his early forties, but he looked so tired. There was something about him that made me believe I could "fix" him. My gut told me this man still had a future with our company. I relished the thought of becoming the corporate hero, the guy who saved Ron and made him a valuable contributor. I knew I could turn him around. So, I hired Ron and we began a journey together. I worked with him day and night for nearly six months. I watched his every move, helped him when he stumbled, and covered up more than a few of his mistakes.

Meanwhile, the morale in my department began to fall. Other engineers came to me and complained about Ron's work. They even went so far as to talk with my section manager about him and my apparent interest in helping him succeed. For me, it was a noble calling. How could I let him fail? After all, I hired him, didn't I?

As you can probably guess, this story does not have a happy ending. In the seventh month, I was called to our division manager's office. He had a few choice words for me. Among them was a new assignment as a senior engineer in another department. He made it clear that I didn't have the stuff of which successful managers are made. My final act as department manager was to terminate Ron. I felt terrible because I had been unfair to him and to the rest of the department. It took me two years to earn back my "stripes" and I vowed that I would learn how to conduct job interviews that would really separate the winners from the rest.

In 1982 I was introduced to an interviewing process that worked. In 1986 I began to seriously study and research this process. Since then, I have worked to make it the most effective interviewing system on the planet. It's all here in this book. It's straight forward and easy to understand. It will help you build a no-nonsense, profit oriented, work team. It will help you avoid hiring mistakes that not only cost you money, but give you plenty of management headaches. Like me, you have probably paid the price once or twice in your career so you know what I'm talking about.

Hiring Mistakes Hurt

Making the right hiring decision is more important today than ever before. I don't have to tell you about the impact of smarter competition and globalization of today's businesses on profits. I'm sure you have felt the pressure. If not, you soon will. Even the smallest company cannot afford to operate as they have in the past and expect to succeed in today's pressure-filled environment. How do you win? You win by building an exceptional work force.

People Make the Difference

Every organization in your line of work has access to comparable locations, equipment, suppliers, and sources of capital. The differentiating factor is the quality of the people who work for you or for your competitors. Doesn't it make sense to select outstanding performers who can make a measurable difference in the bottom line? Don't you want people who have the maturity (i.e., the competence) to help your organization become the pinnacle of success? They're out there. And yes, we are improving productivity through the application of technology, but we will always need great people

Trends and Statistics

Where will these workers come from? According to the Bureau of Labor Statistics:

● The labor force is projected to increase by 17 million workers over the 1998-2008 period from 137 million to 154 million. This represents a significantly lower growth rate than the 17 percent increase over the previous 10-year period, 1988-98. The fastest growing segments will be in the service occupations, along with engineering, and computer professionals.

● The demographic composition of the labor force is expected to change because of shifts in both the population and work force participation.

☐ The labor force age 45-64 will grow faster than the labor force of any other age group as the baby-boom generation (born 1946-64) continues to age. The labor force 25 to 34 years of age is projected to decline by 2.7 million, reflecting the decrease in births in the late 1960s and early 1970s.

☐ The labor force participation rates of women in nearly all age groups are projected to increase. Men's labor force participation rates for 5-year age groups are projected to remain relatively constant, but aggregate participation is projected to continue to decline as the population shifts to older age groups that have lower participation rates. As a result, the women's labor force will grow more rapidly than the men's, and the women's share of the labor force will increase from 46 percent in 1998 to 48 percent in 2008.

☐ The Asian and other labor force and the Hispanic labor force are projected to increase faster than other groups, 40 percent and 37 percent, respectively, because of increased net immigration and higher than average fertility.

☐ The black labor force is expected to grow by 20 percent, twice as fast as the 10 percent growth rate for the white labor force.

☐ The Asian and other share of the labor force will increase from 5 to 6 percent and the Hispanic share from 10 to 13 percent. White non-Hispanics accounted for 74 percent of the labor force in 1998. Their share of the labor force in 2008 will decrease modestly to 71 percent.

☐ By 2008, the Hispanic labor force will be larger than the black labor force.

(Source: Bureau of Labor Statistics)

If the above projections are valid, the labor force will become somewhat more diverse than it is today with women and minorities making moderate headway. Take advantage of these trends by building a more diverse work force. Your customers, your own work force, and your community will look favorably upon your efforts. An added benefit will be your ability to function more effectively in the global marketplace.

You need Good Data to Make Good Decisions

Creating and conducting high quality job-related interviews is not easy. I will show you exactly how to do it. I'll give you some tools to make the process less painful and improve the quality to boot. Research confirms the major weakness with most employment interviews is lack of structure. As a result, these interviews are poor predictors of future job success. Few are conducted properly and outcomes are often less than satisfactory. In this business, we have a saying: "Good data builds good decisions." I will show you how to create a structured interview and how to get good data so you have the opportunity to make good hiring decisions. This is the time to pay the price for learning how to create and conduct employment interviews that will greatly improve your "hit ratio." You will learn how to make the interview less of a "sales" opportunity for the candidate and more of a data gathering opportunity for yourself.

Did you notice I slipped in a little terminology in the last paragraph? I used the words "structured interview." A structured interview is one where the interview questions are pre-written. If you are not currently using structured interviews, you are handicapping yourself. Structured interviews have a much better track record predicting job success than interviews conducted without the aid of pre-written questions. We'll talk about this in a later chapter.

Your "NEW" Role as an Interviewer

Often the employment interview is conducted like a contest where the candidate is attempting to convince the interviewer that he or she has the skills and other necessary qualifications to do the job. Meanwhile, the interviewer is trying to separate fact from fiction, truth from fantasy. The interview takes on the aspects of a "cat and mouse" game. A behavior based interview should be conducted in such a way that the "gamey" aspect becomes an insignificant factor. The purpose of the interview is to gather high quality skill based information. This puts the burden on the interviewer to focus on helping the candidate provide good data in order to reach an optimal hiring decision. The process outlined in this book will help you to conduct systematic, data gathering interviews that get results.

A 7 Step Process

A significant amount of research on employment interviewing has been done in recent years. Key principles from this research have been built into the behavior based interviewing process. *High Impact Hiring* uses a "7 Step" method incorporating the best technology from both research and real world experience. The title of this book could have been: *"How to Create and Conduct a Job-Related Structured Interview That is Legally Defensible, Measures Essential Job Skills, Maintains Respect For The Candidate, is Fair and Focuses on Past Behavior as a Method For Predicting Future Job Success."* A little wordy, don't you think? It might be wordy, but it is indeed accurate. We have learned that much and more from the research. I will share some of these findings with you as we move along and you will come to appreciate the importance of "behavior" versus "personality" in helping you make good hiring decisions.

I have trained many thousands of managers in these techniques in hundreds of workshops over the years. As I mentioned earlier, I first became familiar with this technology in 1982 and have been using and refining it ever since. One thing I know for sure — it works. But it is a *system*. If you use all the pieces you can expect to get outstanding results. When you finish this book, you will have 80% of what you need to conduct high quality employment interviews. The other 20% comes from practice. In any case, you will be pleased with the quality of your interviews. Many previous clients have contacted me to tell me about the compliments they have received from applicants about the professional manner in which the interview was conducted. This does not mean the interviews are "easy." The questions you will ask are tough. To answer these questions, candidates must recall specific events from their past and tell you about them in great detail. It's a rigorous process with a high payoff. I know you will get your money's worth.

This book will show you how to:

- *Build/audit a job description;*

- *Identify essential job functions;*

- *Create a job-related, structured interview;*

● *Get reliable sample of past job-related behaviors;*

● *Systematically evaluate this information;*

● *Select the best person for this job — every time;*

and a lot more!

What you can expect from the "7 Step High Impact Hiring process:

☐ A superior work force that outperforms your competition;

☐ A dramatic reduction in unwanted turnover;

☐ More time to manage your business and lead your people toward your vision and goals;

☐ Fewer performance problems to deal with;

☐ A more impressive bottom line.

As you read through *High Impact Hiring*, you will encounter boxes containing information about suggested activities. These are designed to lead you through the steps that produce high-quality, job-related interviews.

Chapter 2

The Selection Process

The selection process consists of a number of essential activities, the interview is *one* key element. This book focuses primarily on how to prepare and conduct effective interviews. To round out the picture, in this chapter, I have outlined the selection process from the preliminary steps to choosing the best person for the job. Chapter 13 covers post- interview follow up.

Preliminaries

Justify the Need.

Before you add or replace staff, examine the following alternatives:

- Reorganize;

- Analyze current processes to determine which ones can be eliminated or automated;

- Complete a job skills analysis in order to redesign this and other similar positions;

- Conduct technical skills training or team building for existing staff to improve productivity;

- Use overtime or extended hours;

- Transfer employees from other departments on a temporary or permanent basis;

- Contract with an employment agency specializing in temporary workers;

- Hire consultants (outsource).

If these options are not practical, consider the following as you justify the need:

1. What is the downside risk of not creating or filling this position?

2. Is this need the result of a long term increase in workload?

3. To what extent will this job contribute to your overall mission?

4. What are the most essential functions of this position?

5. Who presently performs these functions?

6. Are the employees who presently perform these functions stretched to the limit?

7. How long will it take to make this new employee productive?

8. How will this new position impact your budget?

9. Is there an adequate labor pool from which to choose?

10. Do you have the support of your supervisor and other key people in the organization?

11. If you create or fill this position, will other parts of the organization feel shortchanged?

Define the Job

With the position justified, you will need to collect or develop specifications for the following:

- Job title;

- Primary tasks/duties;

- Responsibilities/Authority;

- Reporting relationships;

- Organization level;

- Qualifications;

- Experience;

- Education;

- Salary range.

Use this information to develop or audit the job description (as outlined in Chapters 5 and 6).

Develop a Structured Interview

The best interviews are those in which the questions, based on a careful job skills analysis, have been written in advance. Research indicates these interviews have the best track record when it comes to selecting the right person for the job (Chapter 7 describes this process in detail).

Attract Potential Candidates

You can't conduct interviews without an adequate supply of job candidates. The following is a list of suggested recruiting tools for you to consider. Your goal is to attract the right candidates. Since you know your organization best, evaluate each of the tools as they relate to your particular situation.

Set up an employee referral program. Many companies have found this to be their most successful method to attract new talent. Friends and family members are known entities and can minimize the risk of making a poor hiring decision.

Advertise in newspapers and trade publications. This probably goes without saying. It's the most obvious way to attract candidates.

Use a limited number of radio spots. Some companies have used this method to reach potential candidates. This is even more costly than newspapers or trade publication advertising. If you have a large number and variety of openings, this is an effective way to attract candidates.

Conduct an open house. An open house is a single employer event held on-site. These are usually held during the evening hours or on weekends and are preceded by advertising. An open house can be limited to a single organization unit such as a department or division or it can be corporate-wide. Your human resources organization can work with you to plan such an event.

Hold a job fair. A job fair is a multi-company event which can include anywhere from 5 to about 50 employers. This event is usually held in a convention center or in a hotel which has large, open ballrooms. Each employer sets up a booth staffed by their representative. The representatives collect résumés, answer questions and distribute company literature such as annual reports, lists of available positions, employment applications and descriptions of benefits.

College recruiting. This option is most often used to supply new college graduates for entry level positions. However, if other sources do not bring in enough candidates, contacting a college placement or alumni association office can often lead you to some highly qualified candidates.

Professional search firms. There are two types of search firms that most companies use: "Retained" firms or "Contingency" firms. Your choice will depend on your needs.

Retained search firms are normally paid a set amount by your organization to find a candidate. They get paid whether they are successful or not. The advantage of using such an organization is obvious; they are usually not in the "body shop" business. They don't toss candidates at you hoping one will stick. They don't have to play a numbers game. Retained search firms can afford to submit candidates who have been carefully screened.

Contingency firms only get paid if you accept one of their candidates. Since this is a commission-only job, it can cost you less in fees but will require more screening on your part.

When you contact an Employment Agency, be sure to inquire about their mode of operation. Find out if they do retained searches, contingency searches, or both. Get some references from them and check them out.

Temporary employment agencies. A visit to the telephone "yellow pages" or a call to your human resources department will put you in touch with a myriad of temporary employment agencies. Many companies have used temporaries as a way to find regular employees. The results however, have been spotty. The advantage is that you can "try before you buy," but the price can be high. Some agencies charge a stiff fee to those companies that hire their employees.

The Internet. When I published the first edition of this book in 1997, there were about 30,000,000 Internet users. According to data provided by *Global Reach* (http://glreach.com) there are now over 300,000,000 Internet users and that number will grow to over 900,000,000 within the next few years. That's a 10X growth in just under four years and a 30X growth in less than eight years. Of these users, nearly half are English speaking. In the United States alone, there are now over 144,000,000 online users.

Since the Internet user population is so large, you need only to access a small portion of the network in order to "place" an ad for a position or to identify who might have the skills you need.

Many organizations have a web site that includes a career or employment section. If this is true of your organization, take full advantage of it. Make sure that it paints a compelling picture of your organization and is not just a place for a potential employee to leave a résumé.

For those of you who are not able to capitalize by using your own organization's web site for recruiting try these web sites:

America's Job Bank (http://www.ajb.dni.us/). This computerized network links the 1,800 state

Employment Service offices. It provides job seekers with the largest pool of active job opportunities available anywhere. For employers it provides rapid, national exposure for job openings. The 'nationwide' listings in America's Job Bank contain information on approximately 250,000 jobs.

The Monster Board (http://www.monster.com). This site offers an extensive listing of job opportunities. Positions in education, government, and private industry are offered along with descriptions of the jobs.

Employment911 (http://employment911.com) Post your jobs to millions of job seekers in one click. Send your jobs to: career web sites, newsgroups, colleges, universities, technical schools, vocational schools and job placement centers.

Jobnet (http://www.jobnet.com). This server is a valuable source of helpful information. Jobnet supplies links to job listings, federal employment opportunities, employment statistics, and detailed descriptions of current job openings.

Vault.com (http://www.vault.com). Vault is one of the Internet's most popular destinations for employers, hiring managers, and HR professionals. Vault.com is a comprehensive free site for employers and it offers the hiring community special targeted content and services to meet the needs of today's employers.

Career Mosaic (http://www.careermosaic.com). This site is one of he best sites on the web for job information. Career Mosaic offers information on some of the top companies in the United States. A job database compiled from news groups is indexed and can be searched for specific job titles. Career search hints are provided in the Library as well as access to the "Employment Directory to North American Markets". A special features section offers offbeat "fun stuff."

HotJobs.com (http://www.hotjobs.com)   In August, 1999, HotJobs.com was rated the number one most recognized job site and sixth most recognized brand of all E-Commerce brands by the *Opinion Research Corporation International*. In addition, HotJobs.com is the only job board to receive a "5-Star" rating by *PC Computing Magazine*.

FlipDog.com (http://www.flipdog.com) FlipDog uses search technology to find jobs that are posted on company web sites. As an employer, you simply direct FlipDog to link to your web site and capture your job listings. You can also manually post jobs on FlipDog's web site at any time.

NOTE: Keeping up with changes in career resources and job listings on the Internet can be a full time job. I recommend you use a search engine such as *Yahoo* (http://yahoo.com) or *Excite* (http://www.excite.com). Enter "jobs" or "employment" as your search term.

Professional associations. Associations such as the Society of Human Resource Managers, the American Marketing Association and the IEEE maintain résumé files and offer referral services to their members. If you are looking for someone in a specific area, you will probably find an appropriate association listed in the Directory of Associations found in most public libraries.

A Special Word About Older Workers

America's workforce is aging along with its population. The pool of 18-24 year old workers will decrease significantly between now and the year 2005. At the same time, the numbers of *potential* workers in the middle and senior age categories will increase dramatically. The problem is that many older workers are taking advantage of early retirement programs put in place to counter short term economic downturns. This is creating a skills drain in some critical manufacturing and service functions.

Older citizens are not just living longer, they are more active and vital than their predecessors. Often, these citizens are ignored when we conduct our recruiting campaigns. As a country, we tend to hire younger workers in the belief that these workers will be the most productive. However, the news is not good when you look at the number of younger people who lack the basic skills needed for employment. Older workers can fill the gap being created by both the growth of jobs (especially in the service sector) and the simultaneous decline of the younger population. Surveys conducted by the American Association of

Retired Persons have noted that most employers have high opinions of older workers and value them for their experience, knowledge, skills, efficiency, productivity, low turnover, commitment, interpersonal skills, maturity, and good accident records.

Screen Potential Candidates

1. Review the application forms and résumés of each potential candidate. Look for information indicating a match with your job requirements.

Carefully review and consider the candidate's:

- Employment objective;

- Summary statement of qualifications and experience;

- Work history;

- Accomplishments listed;

- Titles of jobs held, plus duties and responsibilities;

- Evidence of career progress;

- Length of employment at each job;

- Gaps in dates of employment that are not accounted for;

- Education;

● Non job-related data that gives you information about how this person might fit into your particular work environment.

Remember that résumés are a job candidate's marketing piece. It gives them an opportunity to show themselves in the best light. About one-third of all résumés contain misrepresentations or exaggerations. Make it a practice to verify information shown on the résumé, especially educational credentials.

2. Decide which candidates to bring in for an interview. If necessary, you or your recruiter should telephone the candidates and conduct a preliminary telephone screen. The primary purposes of the telephone screen are to confirm the candidate's interest in the job and to determine if there is a close enough match to bring the person in for an interview. A telephone screen will also give you an opportunity to:

● Verify the candidate's present position, company, duties and responsibilities;

● Verify basic information such as addresses, telephone numbers, dates, and job titles;

● Explore work environment and geographic preferences;

● Get information about most recent projects, accomplishments, changes, etc.;

● Request reference information.

3. Additional information. For those candidates you choose to interview, decide what additional information you need to fill in the gaps in their résumés and how you will obtain this, either before or during the interview.

Interview Candidates and Select the Best

Use the "7 Step" system to interview job candidates and select your primary and backup candidates. Chapter 3 will introduce you to the system. This chapter also contains a review of the most popular interviewing methods in use today. Chapter 4 discusses the unique qualities and advantages of behavior-based interviews. Chapters 5 - 12 describe each of the seven steps in detail.

Chapter 3

Introducing the 7 Steps

How much does a hiring mistake cost you and your company? Thousands of dollars, tens of thousands, hundreds of thousands? In addition to the direct costs of recruiting and hiring, training, salary and benefits, there are indirect costs like loss of personal credibility. I learned my lesson about this when I hired Ron, but it took me two years to gain back the trust and confidence of my manager. I'm sure the rest of my department was also affected. Hire the wrong person and teamwork and morale quickly go down the drain.

One of my clients once confessed : "We never have time to do it right the first time, but we always have the time to do it over." I'm here to help you do it right the first time so you don't have to do it over. This is a pay-me-now or pay-me-later proposition. It takes just a little more effort to do it right the first time and it prevents headaches that come when you replace people more often than is absolutely necessary.

Most organizations believe they only hire the best people and these people out-produce the competition. The truth is, as organizations grow, productivity tends to become more normally distributed and the "people" advantage disappears. Here's the good news: good selection can change this. It's possible to build a truly superior organization by consistently selecting outstanding people. The "7-Step" process will show you how to do it. Everything in the system has been designed to give you results. I have removed the uncertainty and replaced it with a data-driven method that takes the guesswork out of hiring.

The system can be summarized by one seven-letter word — "PROCEED." It's an acronym where each letter represents one step of the process. "PRO-CEED" is your blueprint to interviewing success. You'll be amazed at the results you achieve when you follow this process, step-by-step.

One of the major shortcomings of most job interviews is their lack of predictive validity. We interview candidates for the purpose of predicting who will succeed on the job and who will fail. Poor predictive validity means our interviewing technique is not a useful predictor of future job success. Research confirms that an interview based on a structured process can be a much greater predictor of future job success than an unstructured interview. Interviews that combine structure (where the questions are pre-written) with a careful job skills analysis are even more accurate predictors of job success.

A major strength of the "7 Step" process is its incorporation of both elements (pre-written questions along with a careful analysis of the skills required to do the job).

Following is an overview of the system. Each component will be thoroughly explained in subsequent chapters. Please take a few minutes to familiarize yourself with the "PROCEED" model.

Step 1: PREPARE

☐ Identify existing superior performers

☐ Create a job description for the position

☐ Identify the competencies or skills needed to do the job

☐ Draft interview questions

Step 2: REVIEW

☐ Review questions for legality and fairness

Step 3: ORGANIZE

☐ Select your interview team and your method of interviewing

☐ Assign roles to your team and divide the questions

Step 4: CONDUCT

☐ Gather data from the job candidate

Step 5: EVALUATE

☐ Determine the match between the candidate and the job

Step 6: EXCHANGE

☐ Share data in a discussion meeting

Step 7: DECIDE

☐ Make the final decision

Types of Interviews

In Step 3 above, you are asked to select a method for interviewing job candidates. You have many choices here, but one stands out as the most practical for you and me as practicing managers and professionals. It's called behavior-based interviewing. Before we discuss this method in detail, here's a sampling of some of the other technologies in use today. You could augment the behavior-based approach with the careful addition of one or more of these and get a more complete picture of the match between the candidate's skills and the requirements of the job.

Situational Interview

The interviewer presents the candidate with a series of hypothetical situations and the candidate is asked to describe how they would respond. The interviewer scores each situation using a rating scale based on a set of model answers to the questions. The answer key is based on extensive interviews with existing employees who have been judged by management as being either outstanding, average, or poor performers. Typically, an example is provided for an outstanding response, an average response, and a poor response.

Here's an example from a situational interview for a salesperson selling desktop video projectors:

"Our desktop projectors have high margins, but finding the right customers can be a challenge. If you were hired to sell our products, who would you target as your *primary* customer and why would you do so?"

Expert response: "Specialized audio/visual dealers who design commercial sound and projection systems. These dealers sell directly to large corporate purchasers. The downside is that we're just one of many systems they could carry. However, this channel gives us the greatest exposure and the opportunity to capture a significant market share."

Acceptable response: "Value Added Resellers. These independent business people deal with a large network of end users on a day-to-day basis. They are in a position to know the customer's needs better than anyone else. They respond quickly when customers need technical support and give them personal attention."

Unsatisfactory response: "End users. I'm able to give them the best product to fill their needs. I can work with them if they have budget limitations or technical issues to deal with. I can also get an idea of their future needs and gather information to help us develop new products."

The situational interview has been used very successfully when properly constructed and validated. Its major shortcomings include the need for a fairly large validation sample, costly and time consuming training for interviewers, plus the assistance of an organizational or industrial psychologist (or highly skilled para-professional) to develop the interview.

Simulation/Job Tryout Interview

The job candidate is given a series of tasks to complete that represent actual job conditions. For example:

You hand the candidate a stack of metal and wooden objects, some nuts and bolts, a few hand tools, plus an assembly drawing. You tell the candidate to build the object shown on the assembly drawing. As they do so, you observe the process, noting their manual dexterity, speed, comprehension, and system of logic. You also gather information about their willingness to seek help when necessary and their desire to do quality work. You might also interrupt the task, give the candidate a modified drawing and some new pieces in order to gather evidence about their acceptance or resistance to change.

Simulation gives you the advantage of watching the person demonstrate job-related skills in real time. It takes careful planning however, and may require the use of expensive and complex "props" or special physical surroundings.

Assessment Center

The center is set up either off-site in a special facility run by a consulting firm or within your company. The assessment resembles a simulation except that it has a more complex structure and the evaluation is completed by a team of trained evaluators. For example:

A candidate might spend a full day in an office with a telephone, computer, fax machine, desk, etc. Periodically, the phone rings, people come into the office with various requests, papers and reports are dropped into an in-basket, etc. The candidate must respond to all of these situations, make decisions and take appropriate action. They can be required to prepare and give a presentation to a simulated board of directors or to a hostile customer. All the while, the person is being observed and evaluated.

A special feature of assessment centers is their capability to evaluate a number of candidates simultaneously. They are able to set up leadership and teamwork situations and observe the interaction among job candidates.

The biggest drawback is cost. For some senior positions the investment is justified, but for most jobs the assessment center method is too complex and too time consuming.

Personality or Trait Interview

A trait is a word that is used to summarize a unique quality or characteristic of a person. The trait interviewer is more interested in discovering who the candidate is as a person as compared to a careful analysis of how well the person's skills match the requirements of a job. The trait interviewer wants to understand the psychological makeup of the candidate.

The major problem with trait interviews is their reliance on trait words to describe the unique qualities or characteristics of ourselves and others. For example, a candidate is asked to describe their qualifications. They respond: "My qualifications? Why, I'm great with people, I love a challenge, I'm good at making decisions and getting things done. I'm assertive, tough-minded, and bold."

In day-to-day conversations, this shorthand way of communicating is useful because it saves time. It's efficient, but not effective as an interviewing technique. Labels like these don't reveal anything specific about a person's capabilities. For example, take the word "reliable". To some, "reliable" could mean completing all assignments on schedule. To others, "reliable" means completing one assignment out of three as scheduled.

The meaning we give words come from our experience, and since our experiences are different, so are the meanings of words we use. In addition, many of the labels we use to describe people have positive or negative connotations attached to them. For example, the words "pushy" and "assertive" could be used to describe the same behavior. The choice of a single word could create either a positive or negative impression in the mind of the listener.

I prefer to leave personality or trait interviews in the hands of psychologists or other highly trained specialists. Their well developed skills makes this type of interview useful in certain situations.

Social/Sales Interview

This is the most common type of interview in use today. It doesn't require a great deal of planning on the part of the interviewer. Interview questions are not pre-written and the interviewer relies on his or her social skills to gain information about the candidate's background and experience.

In reality, it takes a skillful interviewer to get the depth of information needed to accurately evaluate the job candidate. Not only does this interviewer need to make the candidate feel comfortable and relaxed at all times, he or she needs to steer the interview in a direction that gets results.

Inexperienced interviewers often default to this type of interview. They find themselves trying to sell the candidate on the benefits of working for them while responding to the candidate's sales pitch. The hiring decision is made on the basis of how well they like the candidate or on their intuition rather than on the evidence of job-related skills.

Cognitive Interview

The cognitive interview is based on the theory that a person's thinking, learning and memory functions are the most crucial factors in determining success on the job. Cognitive interviews often involve a series of tests where practical problems are presented to the job candidate. The methods used to solve these problems are evaluated based on efficiency and effectiveness. The interviewer determines how effectively the job candidate gathers and applies information, what method they use to process data, how they think through alternatives, and a general measure of their mental ability.

Administered by psychologists, these interviews are most useful for jobs with a high degree of intellectual content.

Competency/Critical Incident Interview

The competency interview is closely related to the behavior-based interview. It relies on the ability of researchers to gather behavioral information that can be used to distinguish between superior and ineffective people for a given job.

To establish a list of job competencies, a team of researchers interviews and observes workers on the job. Superior as well as average workers are observed and interviewed and their behaviors are documented. Analysts then identify the competencies or skills which make up the job, focusing on those that differentiate between the superior and average performers. With competencies identified, interpretive guides are developed for the use of interviewers.

Job candidates are brought in and each one is asked to describe critical incidents or situations from their past experience in order to gather information about their skills.

This process is long and time consuming and I have omitted many of the details for the sake of simplicity. It requires a substantial amount of training in order to identify job-related skills and create an appropriate structured interview.

The Behavior-Based Interview

Conducted properly, this interview is the most suitable for interviewers who don't conduct interviews as their life work. The next chapter is devoted exclusively to a discussion of this powerful technology.

Chapter 4

Behavior-Based Interviews

Behaviors are physical actions. In a behavior-based interview, candidates are asked to recall specific actions they have taken in past job-related situations and describe them in detail. For example: If I say, "Jim crossed his arms over his chest," I'm giving you a behavior-based description. On the other hand, if I say, "Jim is angry," I'm interpreting his behavior. I could be right or my interpretation could be highly inaccurate. Perhaps Jim is just tired or bored. He could merely be thinking about something. Fortunately, job skills are made up of behaviors, some of them simple and many of them complex. If you stick with descriptions of behaviors, i.e. describing only specific actions people have taken, you eliminate most of the errors caused by interpretation.

Behavior-based interviews have several outstanding features that make them the ideal choice for most hiring managers:

Behavior-based interviews are structured, thereby insuring each job candidate is treated in a fair and consistent manner.

Based on specific job-related questions, the candidate recalls real experiences and describes these in detail.

Interpretation or assigning meaning to their past experiences by a candidate is eliminated. The candidate simply recreates the experience verbally, describing exactly what took place.

Behavior-based interviews are rich with verifiable data. Candidates are required to include details such as names, dates, times, locations, and numbers.

Candidates are reminded to use the word "I" rather than using "we" or "they" as they describe past experiences. This helps the candidate remain focused on their role in each situation and helps the interviewer evaluate the presence or absence of specific competencies.

Behavior Predicts

Most importantly, behavior predicts. Behavior-based interviews take full advantage of this characteristic. In the behavior-based interview, the interviewer uses examples from the candidate's past to predict future job performance. As it turns out, people are creatures of habit. Once a pattern of behavior is established, a person tends to repeat the pattern again and again. This applies to simple patterns, like tying a shoe lace, to complex work-related patterns such as writing a research report or developing a schematic. Have you ever known someone who always shows up late for a meeting or constantly misses project deadlines? Have you ever tried to change that person's habit? What was the final result?

We do things out of habit because it saves us time and it's comfortable. We don't have to think about how we do things when we do them out of habit. Again, these habits may be efficient for us in the near term, but ineffective in the long run for ourselves as well as for our organizations. The value of behavior-based habits is this: once we have identified them, we can use these patterns to predict future behavior. So, it makes sense for us to ask job candidates questions about past job-related behaviors in order to predict future job performance. This is not to say people don't change over time. I'm sure you're not the same person today you were five years ago. Some of your behaviors have changed, but changes usually come slowly. Behavior-based questions can actually help interviewers track these changes and the lessons candidates have learned from them.

Try this simple exercise: Lay this book down in front of you where you can read the next three steps (go ahead, no one is looking — if they are, they won't know what you're doing anyway).

Step 1: Fold your arms across your chest. Easy, isn't it?

Step 2: Which arm is on top? The left arm or the right arm?

Step 3: Now for the hard part. Unfold your arms and re fold them so the arm that was on top is now on the bottom. How does that feel? Not very comfortable I'll bet.

Do you get the point? We are creatures of habit after all. It's comfortable and easy. And, people become accustomed to our habits. Try sitting in a different chair at the kitchen or dining room table the next time you have an opportunity to do so. Observe the disruption it causes.

Candidates Must Be Trained

Behavior-based information is the principal source of data for the employment interview. Unfortunately, most job candidates don't naturally describe their competencies in behavioral terms. They're used to using trait words to describe themselves and their accomplishments. Following is an illustration of how one interviewer trained a candidate to respond with behavior-based information:

Interviewer: "In your last job as a supervisor, what was one of the most difficult decisions you had to make?"

Candidate: "First of all, let me tell you that I'm very tough-minded. I had to make difficult decisions every day. You don't make it in this business by being a wimp."

> NOTE: The interviewer picks up on the candidate's use of the term "tough minded" and asks for an explanation of how the candidate used this skill in a real situation.

Interviewer: "That's very interesting. Tell me about a time when you were 'tough-minded' in making a difficult decision."

Candidate: "Well, let me put it this way. There were a lot of situations where the rules were pretty vague. I had a lot of headstrong people working for me. My fellow managers were always complimenting me on how well I handled them and gave them clear direction."

> NOTE: The candidate responds with a general description that lacks specificity and does not give the interviewer information about an actual situation. Notice what the interviewer does next.

Interviewer: "Okay, here's what I want you to do. Think about a single incident, one isolated situation where you had a difficult decision to make. Take your time and think of a specific event.

First, describe the SETTING or background.

Next, tell me what ACTIONS you took.

Describe the FINAL OUTCOME.

Then EVALUATE the quality of the end result.

I'm looking for detail so don't hesitate to give me as much information as you can think of."

> NOTE: The interviewer outlines a process for the candidate to follow. The interviewer requests four categories of information in a specific sequence: SETTING — ACTIONS — OUTCOME— EVALUATE. This helps the candidate organize his or her thoughts and gives the interviewer a more complete understanding of how the candidate applied their skills.

Candidate: "Hmm... let me see... oh, okay, here's one. Last March, Red Phillips, he's my boss, came to me and said, 'Look, we've got problems. Sales are down by 30% this quarter and I'm concerned about your overhead. I think you're over-staffed. I want you to review the performance of all your people and let me know by the end of the week which ones you're willing to layoff.' "

NOTE: Notice how the interviewer continues to probe for further details.

Interviewer: "What did you do?"

Candidate: "I said 'Now just a minute Red. What makes you think that laying my people off is going to solve the problem? Every time sales are off, you come to me and give me this layoff baloney.' Well here's what happened next. Red blew his stack! You'd have thought I sold his first-born child! So here's what I did. I said 'Look...' "

Interviewer: "How did it turn out and what did you learn from this situation?"

Candidate: "Well, I never did agree with Red. So, I figured out a way to prove my point. I laid off two of my best people the very next day. I knew that would burn him. Sometimes I think those guys in the front office don't have any idea about what goes on in the real world. Well, he won the battle, but I won the war! I learned that you've go to stand your ground no matter what the boss thinks is best."

NOTE: The candidate "cooked his goose" on this one. It's not uncommon for people to unknowingly give you both positive and negative information about their competencies when describing a specific situation. This is one of the major benefits of using a behavior-based approach to interviewing.

The Response Pyramid

The Response Pyramid™ is a useful tool to help you determine what steps to take in order to get a behavior-based example from the candidate and uncover information about their skills.

The interview described in the preceding pages illustrates the three major levels of the Response Pyramid™.

LEVEL 1 is characterized by the candidate's use of shorthand labels in an attempt to describe skills. There is no specific skill information present in the response. Most candidates respond at this level when

QUALITIES, ATTRIBUTES, CHARACTERISTICS

GENERAL PROCESSES, TESTIMONIAL EVIDENCE

BEHAVIOR-BASED DESCRIPTIONS

Level 1

Level 2

Level 3

they first encounter a behavior-based question. Your job as an interviewer is to train your candidate to give you detailed information about a specific event.

Let's follow the process with an example:

Interviewer: "What qualifies you for this job?"

Candidate: "I'm a good problem-solver. I like to dig into problems and come up with solutions that make a real contribution to the bottom line."

Note: This candidate responds with traits or labels that sound good on the surface, but notice you get no specific information about their skills or competencies.

LEVEL 2 is characterized by a response containing some specifics, but the response still lacks detail. Sometimes the candidate will describe a general process, the end result or simply provide testimonial evidence.

Interviewer: "How do you know you're good at solving problems?"

Candidate: "Last year I successfully handled a lot of difficult situations at work. When I first come across a problem, I try to use a system of cause analysis that I learned in a problem-solving workshop. What we do first is get a handle on the situation and describe it in detail. Next we define the problem in very specific terms. Once we've done that, we start to list possible causes..."

Note: Here's the recipe or description of a general procedure that's characteristic of a Level 2 response. Another problem is the candidate's shift to the use of the word "we" rather than "I". The word "we" can obscure a person's specific role in a situation.

LEVEL 3 is characterized by reference to a *single* event and contains considerable detail. The description of the event includes not only what was done, but exactly where it was done, when it was done, how it was done, and who was involved.

Note: A Level 3 response is specific and rich in detail. It's a right-brain process that requires the candidate to mentally "replay" a single event.

Interviewer: " Tell me about one specific time when you were able to use your problem solving skills. Describe the *Setting in detail. Then tell me what Actions* you took what the *Final outcome* of those actions was, and what you learned *(Evaluate).*"

Candidate: "During the plant shutdown for model changeover last April, a major power failure threatened to close down our new truck assembly line. I got the call from Mike Peters, our plant manager, at 2:15 on a Wednesday morning. I flew out of bed, threw on my clothes and got to the plant in less than 20 minutes. I immediately headed toward our electrical substation to see if the problem was in the plant or on the power company's side of the station. I grabbed a security guard on my way to the substation and had her call the utility company to see if anything was registering on their board. I also stopped by Ed Bradley's office and picked up the maintenance log so I could see what his crew had been doing from the time I left the plant at about 6:00 P.M. on Tuesday..."

NOTE: This interviewer is getting the kind of information he or she needs to decide if this is the right person for the job. Of course a lot more questions need to be asked and answered before a judgment can be made, but the interviewer and the candidate are on the same wavelength. All this interviewer has to do now is ask the right job-related questions, take notes as the candidate responds, and evaluate this candidate's skills following the interview.

Important Reminders

In the chapters that follow, I'm going to show you how the behavior-based interview is merged with the "7 Step" process to give you an unbeatable interviewing system. However, I don't want to move ahead until you have a crystal-clear picture of the key concepts discussed in this chapter.

1. **Behavior predicts**. The best predictor of future behavior is past behavior. Therefore, you need to get detailed behavior-based descriptions of past events in order to determine the extent to which the candidate's competencies match the requirements of the job.

2. **Candidates must be trained**. Do it at the front-end of your interview. You'll save a lot of time if you explain to the candidate what a *Level 3* response is. Give them an example if you can.

3. **Probe for details** as the candidate begins to give you a *Level 3* response to your interview questions. Don't just sit there and listen. If you don't understand something or if you need more information, ask for it.

4. **Get complete data**. The process for getting in-depth information within a *Level 3* response is based on an easy-to-follow formula. Instruct the job candidate to describe the:

> **S**etting or Background;
>
> **A**ctions taken by all parties;
>
> **F**inal Outcome; and an
>
> **E**valuation (what did they learn?)

Use the **SAFE** formula every time you ask for a Level 3 behavior-based example.

An Easy Exercise

Here's an easy and interesting five minute exercise you can do with the help of a friend or colleague. It's an opportunity to experience the process of training a person to give you a *Level 3* response.

Instructions:

Step 1: Explain that you've been reading about an innovative interviewing technique and you would like their help to try it out.

Step 2: Ask this question: "What do you consider to be one of your greatest strengths in dealing with people?" Listen to their reply. They more often than not, you will get a *Level 1* response such as : "I'm good at motivating others."

Step 3: Ask" "How do you know one of your strengths is ...?" Their response will most likely be a *Level 2* "recipe" or testimonial. Example: "My track record proves it."

Step 4: Say: "I'd like you to think about *one* specific situation where you used this skill or ability. First, tell me about the **S**etting or background. Next, tell me about the **A**ctions you took, step-by-step. Then, tell me about the **F**inal outcome and what you learned from this situation (**E**valuate)."

Very Important: Earlier, I said this is a right-brain process. In order for this person to recall a specific situation, they MUST break eye contact with you. When you see this happen, remain silent. Don't interrupt their train of thought. Remember, they need time to come up with a good example for you.

As you listen, remember to guide your friend or colleague through the process, step-by-step. You'll be amazed at the amount of information you get with this simple process.

Let's PROCEED

I introduced the "7 Steps" to you in Chapter 3. Now that you know the behavior-based interview is a critical part of the system, you're equipped to move ahead. If you did the exercise with a friend or colleague, you also have had the opportunity to acquire a key skill needed to conduct high quality, behavior-based interviews.

Now, fasten your seat belt because this is where the real action begins. Before you move on to Chapter 5, select a job, and together we'll build an interview for it. Why? Because, this is a process you must experience. It's like learning to ride a bicycle. Success is more than a matter of simply reading about it. You've got to climb aboard and learn by doing.

 A Second Look at The Road Ahead.
To gain a full and complete understanding of the "7 Step" PROCEED model, you must work with a *real* job. Take a minute to get a specific job in mind. In Chapters 5-7 I will walk you through the procedures to build a high-quality, structured, behavior-based interview. It requires some work on your part. Follow each step carefully. Do each activity as it is presented to you. I promise you, it will be time well spent.

SPECIAL NOTE

Procedures described in Chapters 5-7 may be completed by you working alone. Better results will be realized, however, if you and the members of your interview team work together to complete these tasks. If you are working with a team, it would be helpful for each team member to receive a personal copy of this book.

Chapter 5

Prepare — Part I

In the **PROCEED** model, the letter "P" stands for "Prepare." "Prepare" includes all those activities required to build a job-related, structured interview. You will need to: create a job description, identify the essential job functions, analyze the job and specify the required competencies, develop interview questions, and check your questions for compliance with the law.

In this chapter, you will develop a job description and identify the essential functions. If you already have a written description for this job and the essential functions have been identified, review the next two pages and skip ahead to Chapter 6.

Step One of Seven

Part I —Create a Job Description

If you don't have a current Job Description on file, you will need to develop one. In any case, you should be aware that the *Americans With Disabilities Act* (ADA) requires you to identify the Essential Functions of each job. These are the main functions for which the job was created. It's a term used by the *Equal Employment Opportunities Commission* (EEOC). The EEOC is responsible for the enforcement of the provisions of the *Americans With Disabilities Act*. A carefully written job description prepared *before* advertising a job or interviewing candidates can be used as evidence to support your judgment of what constitutes an Essential Function. By determining which job functions are essential, you will establish a basis for deciding if an individual with a disability is capable of performing the job, or if they could become capable with "reasonable accommodation."

An accurate job description with the Essential Job Functions identified provides the basis for developing a job-related, behavior-based interview that is legally defensible. A good job description also gives you the tools you need to guide your search for applicants, makes it easier to screen applications and résumés, and saves you time in the interviewing process. It provides an accurate and complete picture of the job to the applicant and helps them understand exactly what will be expected should they be hired. Finally, if a hiring decision you make is challenged by an applicant, employee, or government agency, you will find it much easier to respond to inquiries about the Essential Functions of a job, qualification requirements, or working conditions.

Questions you ask during an employment interview must be job-related and must not discriminate either intentionally or unintentionally against any person or group of people protected by the *Americans With Disabilities Act of 1990, the Civil Rights Acts of 1964 and 1991* or certain other regulations. Also, you must be able to demonstrate questions you ask are linked to Essential Functions of the job and are supported by business necessity.

> NOTE: In subsequent chapters I discuss how to develop a draft of your job-related structured interview and audit it for fairness and compliance with the law.

How To Create A Job Description

Use the format developed by your organization or a copy of *page 1* of the *Job Description Planner* located in Appendix A, pages 229-231. The following information will be needed if you want to complete the entire *Job Description Planner*:

☐ Job Title;

☐ Main Purpose;

☐ Job Functions and Associated Competencies;

☐ Experience, Education and Training;

☐ Reporting Relationships, Special Requirements or Other Information.

Information to help you develop each section follows.

Job Title. The job title should identify the job content, purpose, and scope in as few words as possible. It should communicate the type and level of work performed. Here are some helpful hints:

☐ Create or select titles that are common to your industry or your organization;

☐ Use accurate titles (Don't call a custodian a maintenance engineer!);

☐ Titles should not be confusing regarding exemption from the Fair Labor Standards Act (Pay or no-pay for overtime).

> *Example:* Programmer, personal computers, data base applications.

Main Purpose. Briefly describe the job's primary purpose (its mission). Highlight the job's general characteristics. Provide enough information to distinguish this job from others in your organization. Make it brief, clear and accurate. Follow these guidelines:

☐ Limit the description of purpose to about 50 words;

☐ Use words that are clear and unambiguous;

☐ Use action verbs to describe the major elements of the job.

Example: The main purpose for this job is to write complete data base software applications for in-house personal computer users. Responsibilities include all phases from receiving user requests, project planning and design, writing code, testing code, final installation, and on-going program maintenance for all users.

To Do:
1. On a blank sheet of paper, duplicate the layout of page 1 of the Job Description Planner from Appendix A, page 229.
2. Record the Job Title and the Main Purpose on your copy of page 1 of the Job Description Planner.

Job Functions for this position. List functions, duties, and responsibilities for the job. Cover all the key performance areas. Follow these guidelines:

☐ List functions in some logical sequence based on order of importance, sequence, or interdependence;

☐ Be specific rather than general — avoid using vague or ambiguous terms;

☐ Don't attempt to create an exhaustive list, focus on the major functions (6 to 15 statements will be adequate for most jobs);

☐ Begin each statement with an action verb.

Example:

1. Converts data from project specifications and statements of problems and procedures to create or modify computer programs.

2. Prepares or receives from Systems Analyst detailed work flow charts and diagrams to illustrate the sequence of steps that a program must follow and to describe input, output, and logical operations involved.

3. Analyzes work flow chart and diagrams, applying knowledge of computer capabilities, subject matter and symbolic logic in order to create efficient applications.

4. Confers with supervisors and representatives of departments concerned with the program to resolve questions of program intent, data input, output requirements, and inclusion of internal checks and controls.

5. Converts detailed logical flow charts to data base programs which can be processed by the computer.

6. May train users of the program in order to insure they are able to effectively apply it to their situation.

7. May assist the user to resolve problems in running computer programs on their hardware.

> **To Do:**
> Identify and record the Job Functions on your copy of page 1 of the Job Description Planner for the job you are working with .

Classify Job Functions. Indicate which functions are *Essential* or *Non-essential*. The ADA considers job functions *Essential* if:

☐ The reason the position exists is to perform that function;

☐ There are only a limited number of employees available among whom the performance of that function can be distributed;

☐ The function is so highly specialized that the person in the position is hired for his or her expertise or ability to perform the particular function.

The ADA regulations list the following types of information that can be considered in determining whether a job function is essential:

☐ Work experience of past incumbents in a job;

☐ Current work experience of incumbents in similar jobs;

☐ Amount of time spent on the job performing the function;

☐ The effect of removing the function from the job;

☐ Terms of a collective bargaining agreement.

Use of the following ADA guidelines may help you decide if a job function is essential:

The job function is probably **ESSENTIAL** if:

---

1. This position exists in order for the job function to be performed. It is obviously related to the central purpose of the job.

2. This function is being performed during the vast majority of time the person is on the job.

3. There are clear negative economic or safety consequences if the function is not performed.

4. Personnel practices, precedents, job descriptions, and other documentation suggest this function is essential.

The job function is probably **NON-ESSENTIAL** if:

1. This function is related to a secondary purpose of the job.

2. This function does not require a significant amount of time.

3. There are minimal negative consequences if this function is not performed.

4. The function could be performed equally well by people of varying aptitudes, interests, and work styles.

To Do:
See Appendix A, page 229 for a completed example of page 1 of the Job Description Planner. Note that the Essential Functions have been identified. Using the guidelines just presented and using your best judg- ment, make a checkmark to indicate those functions that are essential to the job you are working on.

The ability to perform non-essential job functions should *not* be used to determine if a job candidate will be hired. It's not necessary for you to make these functions part of your job description. If you are go- ing to include them, be sure to list them separately from the Essential Job Functions and clearly identify them as Non-Essential.

Note: One way to maintain flexibility in your job descriptions is to replace or supplement a list of Non-Essential job function with this statement: "Other non-essential duties and responsibilities may be assigned to this po- sition from time to time."

Chapter 6

Prepare — Part II

At this point you have identified the *Essential Functions* for a particular job. To complete your job description:

- Specify the competencies required to perform these functions;

- Add details about experience, education, special requirements, and any other information you feel is relevant.

With the job description completed, you have a solid foundation for developing your structured behavior-based interview.

Step One of Seven — Continued

Part II — Specify Competencies

Two basic classes of competencies are fundamental components of any job: *Technical Skills* and *Work Habits.*

Technical Skills

Technical Skills make up the content of the job. These describe WHAT knowledge or abilities are required to perform the essential job functions. Technical skills can be learned on the job through training and experience, or through classes taught in vocational schools or in traditional educational institutions. Some Technical Skills are cognitive in nature while others require the use of tools, equipment, or instruments. Others require physical action on the part of the job holder.

Technical Skills are easy to identify. If you are familiar with the job, you most likely know what Technical Skills are required to accomplish it. A few examples of Technical Skills are: writing computer programs, balancing the books the end of the month, operating machine tools, changing a flat tire, dressing a wound, flying an airplane, making change for a customer, or assembling a personal computer.

The next step in creating your job interview is to identify the Technical Skills required to perform each job function. The following is an example from our Personal Computer Programmer job.

Essential Job Function: Prepares or receives from Systems Analyst detailed work flow charts and diagrams to illustrate the sequence of steps that a program must follow and to describe input, output, and logical operations involved.

Technical Skills: Creates logic diagrams and flow charts that utilize the benefits of object oriented programming in order to develop fast and efficient programs. Reads and interprets complex flow charts and diagrams.

See page 2 of the sample Job Description Planner in Appendix A, page 230 for more examples.

To Do:
1. On as many blank sheets of paper as you need, duplicate the layout of page 2 of the Job Description Planner from Appendix A.
2. List the Essential Job Functions for your targeted job on these new pages.
3. List the Technical Skills required to perform each Essential Job Function.

NOTE: It is neither necessary or desirable to specify the exact method used to perform a task . The emphasis should be placed on the outcome or purpose since a disabled person may be able to achieve the same result by using a different method.

Work Habits

Work Habits, in contrast to Technical Skills, describe HOW the person performs the job. These skills may apply to many different jobs and help determine how well the person will function in your particular work environment. They are reflections of a person's beliefs, attitudes, and values about the work to be done and are learned through life experience. Most interviews focus on assessing a job candidate's technical abilities and fail to take into consideration the importance of Work Habits as a determining factor in success on the job. Many people who don't succeed in an organization (they get fired or they quit) do not fail because they lack Technical Skills. They fail because, for one reason or another, they don't have the appropriate Work Habits. Perhaps they are too bureaucratic or maybe even too flexible. They may lack commitment or are unable to work in a team environment. Possibly they cannot set priorities, cope with stress, or react appropriately in emergencies.

Identifying Work Habits

Following is a list of 35 Work Habits that apply to most jobs.

☐ **Acumen:** Ability to deal effectively with organizational politics and build alliances with people at all organizational levels.

☐ **Adaptability:** Ability to demonstrate flexibility in dealing with difficult or unpleasant circumstances, or adjusting to changing conditions, in order to meet job requirements.

☐ **Analysis:** Ability to gather information and extract relevant data and apply it to a current situation in order to arrive at a conclusion, solve a problem, or make a valid decision.

☐ **Assertiveness:** Ability to express oneself in a confident manner and maintain a point of view even while experiencing opposition.

☐ **Coaching:** Ability to evaluate the development needs of employees and provide guidance in improving current job performance or preparing for career advancement.

☐ **Collaboration:** Ability to work effectively with others in order to achieve meaningful results.

☐ **Commitment to Quality:** Ability to champion the need to deliver quality products and services; to maintain the issue of quality as a primary organizational focus, and to support the concept of "Total Quality Management".

☐ **Compliance:** Ability to follow established guidelines, policies, and procedures in order to insure consistency or to protect the safety or preserve the welfare of others.

☐ **Conflict Management:** Ability to work with people at all levels in the organization to create effective solutions and maintain positive working relationships when disagreements arise.

☐ **Critical Thinking:** Ability to examine information, facts, and data, and make valid judgments based on content and quality.

☐ **Customer Satisfaction:** Ability to build productive relationships with internal or external customers in order to build customer loyalty and business success.

☐ **Decision Making:** Ability to systematically evaluate the positives and negatives of competing choices in order to select the most appropriate alternative.

☐ **Decisiveness:** Ability to make a decision based on available information and assume the risks involved in order to achieve a desired result.

☐ **Dedication:** Ability to fully invest oneself in the job and exhibit a high level of commitment; often makes personal sacrifices in order to get the job done or to handle a temporary increase in workload.

☐ **Empathic Listening:** Ability to listen attentively and to fully and deeply understand a person on an emotional as well as an intellectual level.

☐ **Empowerment:** Ability to build a workplace culture in which people take personal responsibility for making themselves and their organization successful.

☐ **Goal Setting:** Ability to set goals for oneself or others that are realistic, time bound, describe the desired result, comprehensive, and stated plainly enough to be understood.

☐ **Information Management:** Ability to evaluate the requirements of the organization for information and to provide information on a timely basis.

☐ **Influence:** Ability to persuade others to take a course of action or to alter their opinions in the absence of direct authority over them.

☐ **Innovation:** Ability to generate creative or original solutions to apply to new and existing situations or to tap the creative genius within one's people or customers.

☐ **Integrity:** Ability to maintain firm adherence to values and principles even in the face of significant pressure to compromise.

☐ **Leadership:** Ability to establish a meaningful vision that defines organizational purpose and through exemplary behavior, expertise, and personal power, directs the thinking and actions of others in order to achieve the desired result.

☐ **Managing Change:** Ability to initiate, implement and promote change in the organization in order to create new business opportunities, meet market demands, develop new technology, respond to customer or employee needs, or maintain continuous improvement efforts.

☐ **Managing Diversity:** Ability to recognize and effectively employ differences among people in a manner that demonstrates respect for the individual while at the same time achieving the required result.

☐ **Motivation:** Ability to create a desire in others to perform at a high level or to modify their attitudes through the use of role modeling, positive reinforcement, and incentives.

☐ **Organizing:** Ability to develop an effective organizational structure, recruit and hire a competent staff, and develop systems, processes, and procedures in order to achieve high quality output.

☐ **Planning and Scheduling:** Ability to develop short and long range plans that are comprehensive, realistic, and effective in achieving established objectives.

☐ **Problem Solving:** Ability to systematically organize and evaluate information in order to determine the true cause of a problem and apply corrective action.

☐ **Sociability:** Ability to approach and interact with others in a warm, friendly, and supportive manner, creating a climate of trust, consideration and mutual respect.

☐ **Spoken Communications:** Ability to effectively present ideas, transmit information, or convey concepts to individuals or groups of people of varying educational, cultural and experience levels.

☐ **Strategic Thinking:** Ability to use information about the organization, competition, and market conditions to identify and develop plans to accomplish the goals of the organization.

☐ **Team Building:** Ability to help a work group use all of its resources and expertise to manage complex situations and achieve positive results.

☐ **Versatility:** Ability to temporarily modify one's social style in order to meet the needs of others without sacrificing personal integrity.

☐ **Vigilance:** Ability to recognize changes in the physical environment in order to alter a course of action or apply corrective measures.

☐ **Written Communications:** Ability to present ideas and convey information clearly and effectively through formal and informal documents; edits, interprets, and reviews written works by self and others.

Clearly, all these Work Habits don't apply to the job you are working with. To determine the critical Work Habits that apply to a given job, complete the Work Habits Analysis which follows.

Work Habits Analysis

The purpose of this analysis is to:

- Reduce the number of Work Habits to a manageable level, then to

- Identify Work Habits that separate superior performers from average performers. If you focus on these key competencies, you will build an organization that consistently out performs all others.

Work Habits are divided into two categories:

- Threshold Competencies; and

- Differentiating Competencies.

Threshold Competencies include *all* Work Habits that are part of a job. These are the *baseline* competencies needed to perform both essential and non-essential job functions. In a perfect world, you would select only job candidates who have Work Habit skills that satisfy all baseline job requirements.

Differentiating Competencies are those few highly developed Work Habits separating breakthrough performers from average performers. These competencies hold the key to building high performance organizations. These Work Habit skills along with Technical Skills become the primary focus of your employment interviews.

To Do:
Step 1: Identify Baseline Competencies. (Approximately 15-20 baseline competencies are required for most jobs). From the listing on pages 80 to 86, select all those Work Habits that make up the job and record you selections on a blank sheet of paper.

Step 2: Identify Differentiating Competencies. From your list of baseline competencies, select 6 to 8 Work Habits that separate beakthrough performers from average performers. Here are some questions to guide your final selection:

Who are the superior performers among your present job holders?

What Work Habits do they have that set them apart from average performers?

What other Work Habits are needed to do this job in an outstanding manner?

If you are like most interviewers, you might be reluctant to narrow your Work Habit selections to only six or eight. Remember, your goal is to select superior performers and you have only a limited amount of time to conduct each interview. It will take you at least 30 minutes to gather enough data from a job candidate to evaluate these Work Habits. If you add the amount of time required to build rapport with the candidate, explore Technical Skills, sell your organization, answer questions and handle other administrative issues, I'm sure you can see just how difficult it is to conduct a complete interview in an hour or less. You will lose very little by concentrating on your key Work Habits. You will get 99% of the data you need to accurately assess a job candidate's competencies if you limit your questions to those related to a few critical areas.

Link Key Work Habits to Essential Job Functions

According to Equal Employment Opportunities Commission (EEOC) guidelines, when you have identified key Work Habits, you should link them to Essential Job Functions.

> Note: Work Habits often apply to more than one Essential Function. Therefore, it is not unusual to have multiple entries in your Job Description Planner for a single Work Habit.

To Do:
Add Work Habits to your Job Description Planner. For an example see Appendix A, page 230.

It probably seems like you have done a lot of work just to arrive at the point where you can develop questions for a job interview. Well, you have! More importantly, you have established a solid procedural and legal foundation for your interview questions.

Most interviewers don't take the time to properly prepare for their interviews. As a result, their interviews lack structure and they find themselves constantly struggling to conduct high quality interviews that give them reliable information.

Complete Your Job Description Planner

Experience, education and training. This is the place to list degree, certificate or license requirements, job-related experience, or any special training requirements.

> NOTE: It is not legal to require a degree from a college or university without allowing equivalent experience. Therefore when you complete this section, be sure to include the words " or equivalent experience" if you believe a degree is necessary.

Reporting relationships. Identify the Job Title to whom this job reports. List Job Titles of subordinate positions.

Special requirements. These include travel, environmental considerations, physical requirements, time constraints or other factors not previously listed.

These criteria take on special significance if challenged under state or federal employment laws. Therefore, it is important they are not overstated or irrelevant. You are obligated to show they are job related and the result of business necessity. It is a good idea to keep notes on any special requirements if the rationale for their inclusion is not obvious.

> NOTE: You cannot use hiring standards that discriminate against someone with a disability unless you have a legitimate business reason for doing so. You must have these standards validated by a professional Industrial Psychologist or through careful observation by in-house job experts.

To Do:
Add the Experience, Education and Training, Reporting Relationships, and Special Requirements to your Job Description Planner.

Check Your Work

This is a good time to stop and check your job description for legality and completeness before you move on. In most organizations, a job description is created by the immediate supervisor and then reviewed by human resources or legal staff. It's important to have at least two other people involved in order to ensure that the job description meets the organization's need for consistency with other positions, treats people fairly, and complies with the law. Determining who will check your work depends upon the structure of your organization and to whom these responsibilities have been assigned. If you don't have a legal or human resources function in your company, you might consider consulting a labor relations attorney or other specialist.

At a minimum your review should include consideration of the following:

☐ A job description should comply with existing human resource policies and guidelines;

☐ A job description should not contain requirements which may discriminate on the basis of:

RACE

SEX/GENDER

RELIGION

NATIONAL ORIGIN

COLOR

AGE

MILITARY SERVICE

CITIZENSHIP

DISABILITY

Note: A job description should avoid eliminating candidates with disabilities that could be accommodated without causing undue business hardship or endangering others (see page 123 for a discussion of Reasonable Accommodation).

Chapter 7

Prepare — Part III

Step One of Seven — Continued

I'll bet you're saying to yourself,

> "Prepare — Part III? Aren't we finished yet? I mean — nearly a third of this book is devoted to a single topic..."

As you can see by now, creating and conducting interviews that get results involves a lot more than most people realize. Fortunately, it's a high-payoff activity. Once the preparation phase is done and a structured behavior-based interview has been built for a specific job, this step doesn't have to be repeated unless the job requirements change significantly. Store your completed interview in your filing cabinet or desk drawer and make photocopies as you need them. Then you can reap the rewards of your hard work over-and-over again.

Develop experience based questions

To assess a candidate's job-related knowledge, skills, and abilities, develop a series of open-ended questions for each Work Habit and Technical Skill you have identified.

The most comprehensive question development process requires three steps:

- Create draft questions;

- Evaluate questions for fairness and legality;

- Refine questions as necessary.

Step 1 is the subject of this chapter. Steps 2 and 3 will be covered in Chapter 8.

Create a draft of your questions

At this point, you should have a completed job description (or Job Description Planner). You have identified the competencies needed to perform each essential job function. Now you're in a position to create open-ended questions that are directly linked to each skill or competency.

Schematically, the process looks like this:

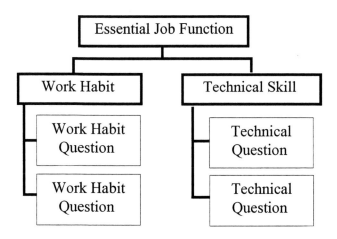

In this illustration, only one Work Habit and one Technical Skill have been tied to the Essential Job Function. In reality, several Work Habits and Technical Skills will be required to fulfill the requirements of an Essential Job Function.

> NOTE: The number of questions you need is a function of the number of interviewers who will assist you in the hiring process. Each interviewer will require at least two questions for each Work Habit and Technical Skill you have identified as important for a job. For example, if you are using two other people to help you with interviews, you will need a total of six questions for each Work Habit and Technical Skill.

Work Habit Questions

Since Work Habits play such a vital role in determining who will succeed and who will fail in a given job, I'll focus our attention on this set of competencies first. Let's select, edit, and create the Work Habit questions that make up your structured interview. Then we'll turn our attention to the writing of Technical Questions.

Selecting Work Habit Questions. I've made this task easier by providing 175 pre-written questions for you to use as examples to help build your structured interview. These are located in Appendix C, pages 256-290.

To do.
Complete this sequence for each key Work Habit:
Step 1: In Appendix C, locate the page with the definition of the Work Habit at the top.
Step 2. Scan the list of pre-written interview questions and select two or three that are relevant to the job.
Step 3. Based on your knowledge and experience, modify the questions to reflect specific requirements of the job. Use words that match your style of communicating.

When you have completed the exercise above, you will have a collection of between 12 and 24 Work Habit questions to include in your structured interview. Unless you are the only person interviewing job candidates, this will not be enough. You will need at least two questions per Work Habit for each member of your interviewing team. Where will these additional questions come from? You'll create them using some additional aids I have provided for you.

How to Create Additional Work Habit Questions

You will use the same process to create questions I used when I developed the initial 175 samples. To do this, you will use the *complete* Work Habit definitions located in Appendix B. These definitions include a list of "elements" that add considerable depth to the brief definitions you previously used to select your six to eight key Work Habits.

Here's an example to help you get started. I've copied some information from Appendix B, page 238 to help illustrate this process.

When I want to create a new question, I read the one-sentence definition first:

> **Coaching** — Ability to evaluate the development and needs of employees and provide guidance in improving current job performance or preparing for career advancement.

After reading the definition, I scan the "elements" which are listed immediately following it:

- Able to recognize job holder's areas of strength as well as areas where development is needed;

- Encourages job holder to be proactive in improving their performance or preparing for advancement;

- Provides challenging and meaningful assignments;

- Creates the proper conditions which foster professional growth;

- Assists employees in building a development plan;

- Suggests resources such as potential mentors and training opportunities;

- Provides employees with information about available positions in the organizations that are consistent with the employee's career goals;

- Gives employees opportunities to be exposed to other parts of the organization;

- Monitors day to day work performance and provides regular performance feedback to job holders;

- Gives employees feedback that is specific and behavior-based rather than judgmental;

● Does not often punish mistakes; instead, uses them as opportunities for problem solving.

Next, I select one element from the definition that reflects a job requirement. Let's assume I focus on:

"Provides challenging and meaningful assignments"

Finally, I write an "open-ended" question that requires the candidate to recall a specific event related to the selected element.

Example: "Tell me about a time when you gave a subordinate a particularly difficult or challenging assignment. To what extent was that a positive or negative experience for this person?"

The Power of Open-Ended Questions

The questions I write are open-ended. These questions give the candidate an opportunity to recall a specific event from their work or life experience and to describe that experience in detail. Here are some key phrases I use to begin many of my open-ended questions:

Recall a situation where...

Tell me about a time...

What have you done when...

Give me an example from your background...

Questions beginning with these kinds of phrases encourage the candidate to talk and gives them permission to include the specifics you need to evaluate their competencies. Closed-ended questions limit the amount of information you can get because they require short answers, often just one or two words.

Following are a few examples of closed-ended questions:

> "Have you ever felt that your boss asked too much of you?"

> "When was the last time you used your ability to solve a difficult problem?"

> "Have you ever had a conflict with a co-worker?"

Closed-ended questions can paralyze you. Inexperienced interviewers often find themselves trapped by asking a series of closed-ended questions that give them little, if any, useful information.

Look what happened to this interviewer:

Interviewer: "Jane, your résumé says you majored in organizational psychology in college. Did you take a class in the study of individual differences?"

Candidate: "Yes."

Interviewer: "Did you learn how to identify social styles in that class?"

Candidate: "Yes, I did."

Interviewer: "What model did you use?"

Candidate: "It was based on Jung's work. I remember it was a four-quadrant model."

Interviewer: "Did your instructor talk about how to resolve conflicts between people with different styles?"

Candidate: "Yes, she did."

Interviewer: "When did you take that class?"

Candidate: "Two years ago."

Interviewer: "How well did you do?"

Candidate: "Great. I got an A-."

Interviewer: " Oh, one other thing. Did you learn how to use paper and pencil inventories to identify a person's social style or personality?"

Candidate: "Yes."

Interviewer: "Have you had experience in administering these inventories or have you just studied them?"

Candidate: "I've had experience in administering and interpreting them."

Interviewer: "How many times have you administered inventories like this?"

Candidate: "Probably 40 to 50 times."

Interviewer: "Good. Which one have you had the most experience with?"

Candidate: "I think the Gordon Personal Profile."

Interviewer: "Have you ever run into a person who made it difficult for you to administer a personality inventory?"

Candidate: "Maybe once or twice."

Interviewer: "Jane, how would you rate yourself on a 10 point scale regarding your ability to administer inventories under such conditions? One is poor and ten is excellent."

Candidate: "I'd have to say either an eight or a nine".

Interviewer: "Very good."

> NOTE: The interviewer has to work very hard to get data due to the limitations of closed-ended questions. The information our interviewer obtained in the previous example is neither complete, clear, nor very useful.

Why not ask the candidate an open-ended question that gives them the opportunity to recall a specific experience or group of experiences? Our interviewer could have asked a question like this:

Interviewer: "Jane, your resume indicates you majored in organizational psychology in college. Summarize the work you did as you studied individual differences."

Candidate: "Well, Dr. Collins, I had the opportunity to do a considerable amount of study in this area. My most recent contact with individual differences was in a graduate assessment and testing class. I had the opportunity to look at many instruments, the

Myers-Briggs, the Millon Index of Personality Styles, the Sixteen Personality Factor Questionnaire, the Gordon Personal Profile and several others."

> NOTE: The interviewer can get more specific information by following up with another open-ended question.

Interviewer: "Jane, tell me about the most challenging situation you faced in administering and interpreting one of these instruments."

Candidate: " Okay. Last year I had the opportunity to work in the Lemon Heights clinic as part of my internship. A lady came in to apply for a technical assistant's position. I was asked to administer the Gordon Personal Profile. The profile measures eight personality traits that are important to daily functioning. As I began to talk with this lady, I noticed she seemed very uneasy about taking the inventory. I decided, I'd better find out what was going on before I continued, so here's what I did..."

> NOTE: This interviewer is now in a position to get a great deal of useful information about this candidate's skills. As you recall, the last question elicits a *Level 3* response from the candidate. The interviewer can probe deeper into the example to gain more specific and in-depth data.

To do:
WRITING WORK HABIT QUESTIONS
Step 1. Select a Work Habit from those listed in your Job Description Planner and locate the appropriate definition in Appendix B.
Step 2. Scan the skill elements beneath the definition and choose one that is linked to a job requirement.
Step 3. Write one or more open-ended questions that require the candidate to recall specific events related to the selected element.
Step 4. Repeat the process as necessary until you have two questions per interviewer for each Work Habit.

Let's move on to the technical questions and complete "Prepare."

Technical Questions

Behavior-based questions focus primarily on a job candidate's real-world experiences. These experiences are the best predictors of future job success. However, since Technical Skills are often based on a body of knowledge, education, or specialized training, consider asking some "What-If" questions, "How-To" questions or "Knowledge-Dependent" questions to supplement your behavior-based questions.

What-if questions present the candidate with a hypothetical situation and test a candidate's ability to respond with the most effective course of action.

Example: "A patient comes to you complaining of severe pain in her lower back. She tells you it started last night as she stood up from the dinner table. When she tried to walk the pain was intense enough to cause her a great deal of discomfort. When she went to bed that night, the pain subsided. She slept through the night without waking. As she arose in the morning, the pain returned and its intensity increased as she walked to the bathroom. When she sat down to breakfast, the pain eased somewhat. As she rose to leave the table, the intensity of her pain increased substantially. At this point, she contacted her daughter to drive her to your office. What might her problem be and what questions would you ask to complete your diagnosis?"

How-To questions often reveal the candidate's depth of knowledge in a specialized area. Examples:

"How do you calculate the amount of deflection in a steel beam under load?

"How do you troubleshoot a cruise control that operates but is erratic or unstable?"

"What steps should a technician take to insure that cache memory chips are correctly installed?"

Knowledge-Dependent questions require the candidate to apply specific knowledge or training to answer correctly. Examples.

"How long must a scuba diver remain at a decompression stop after 20 minutes at a depth of 140 feet?"

"What are the major causes of failures in high voltage transformers?"

"Identify the three most abundant species of fish found on the Atlantic Ocean side of South Africa."

"What are the primary components of an automotive air conditioner?"

"Calculate the amount of capital gains taxes due based on the following transactions..."

NOTE: While "What-If", "How-To", and "Knowledge-Dependent" questions are useful for assessing technical competencies, I recommend you avoid using them for gathering data about Work Habits. Since past behavior is the best predictor of future behavior, stick to behavior-based questions as you examine a job candidate's Work Habits.

Sample Technical Skills Questions

The following is a sample of some Technical Skills questions used in an interview for a Personal Computer Programmer in an Information Systems department. The position provides support for internal users who have applications that can best be served by creating user-specific programs.

Project Design: Able to convert problem statements into project specifications in order to solve the user's problem.

> Question 1. A "Project Specification" is the unifying mechanism that gathers the pieces of an application together. What are the key ingredients of a well formulated project specification?.

> Question 2. Think about a project that you recently completed. Explain how you went about converting problem statements and user needs into project specifications.

Program Design: Converts project specifications and flowcharts into a program design and plan including choices about user interface, programming language and multi-user considerations.

> Question 1. Describe the process you use to design a computer program once the project specifications have been developed and documented.

> Question 2. What information is contained in a work flow chart and how is this information used to influence program input, output and logic?

> Question 3. Briefly summarize your experience in preparing work flow charts and logic diagrams.

Question 4. What techniques do you use to estimate the time and effort required to complete a program once the design has been established?

Question 5. How do you determine which language is appropriate for a given application? Tell me about one of your most recent experiences in making such a choice.

Question 6. What configurations for LANs are you most familiar with? What factors determine which configuration to use in a given situation?

Question 7. What determines if an application is more appropriate for a WAN vs. a LAN?

Writing Code: Able to write code that includes specified functionality in a multi-tasking environment.

Question 1. Explain the process you use to translate flow chart/logic diagrams into code segments.

Question 2. What safeguards are most often used to prevent unknown references from crashing a program?

Question 3. An application might need certain resources to run such as specific files, a certain amount of memory or disk space and so on. Which functions do you typically build into your applications to check these resources?

Question 4. What are some of the problems encountered when using low-level file functions in PC based applications?

Question 5. Have you ever implemented DDE in any of your PC based applications? If so, give me an example of how you used either a macro or a programming language to initiate DDE.

Question 6. What programming strategy would you use to build a DDE client application as opposed to a DDE server application?

Integrating Segments Into an Application: Designs and writes blocks of code that can be integrated into an application.

Question 1. Files referenced in an application can be either executable or non-executable. How do you determine which of these are most appropriate for a given application?

Question 2. An application can have many segments (or "Projects") or only one. What factors determine how many segments ("Projects") an application should have?

Question 3. Explain the advantages and shortcomings of using embedded OLE objects in an application.

Question 4. Under what circumstances would OLE object linking be preferred over OLE embedding?

NOTE: A "question" is not limited to a single statement. It's often helpful to the job candi- date to supply a "lead-in" sentence that puts the question in proper context.

To do:
Writing Technical Questions
Step 1. For each Technical Skill listed in your copy of the Job Description Planner pages, use your technical job knowledge to create a variety of questions to give you data about the skill. Include "Behavior-Based", "What-If", "How-To", and "Knowl- edge-Dependent" questions as appropriate. Remember to write at least two questions per interviewer for each Technical Skill.

Step 2. Critique your questions. Are they logical? Do they contain jargon? Is there a correct answer or range of answers? Do they vary in degree of technical knowledge or skill level? Are they too complex for a job candidate to handle during an interview?

Guidelines. Here are some guidelines to help you build high-quality technical questions:

☐ Avoid theoretical or philosophical questions with no direct relationship to what is done on the job;

☐ Develop as many behavior-based questions as you can in order to reveal the candidate's actual work experience or knowledge as it relates to the skills being assessed, use "What-If," "How-To," or "Knowledge-Dependent" questions to supplement these;

☐ Provide sample answers to technical questions to be used by anyone who assists you in interviewing job candidates;

☐ Keep your technical questions free of terms and jargon that are not common to the job, your industry, or type of organization;

☐ Use internal operating manuals, publications, and technical documents as resources to help develop job-related technical questions;

☐ Create questions that measure different degrees of Technical Skill from elementary to advanced;

☐ Test your questions on current and former job holders before you use them in employment interviews.

If you've done your homework, you now have a collection of Work Habit and Technical Skill questions for your structured interview. If you are the only person conducting interviews, you most likely have selected or written about 12 to 24 Work Habit questions and 16 to 30 Technical Skill questions. If you have one or more colleagues to help you interview, you will have two or three times as many.

You now have a draft of a powerful, job-related interview. You began by creating a job description and identifying the essential functions. Your skills analysis and interview questions have been carefully linked to these essential functions.

Congratulate yourself. You have just completed the most difficult and time consuming part of the "7 Step" process. From this point on, we pick up speed.

In the next chapter, you will examine some of the legal issues affecting the employment interview. I'll ask you to review your pre-written interview questions and re-word or eliminate those that are illegal or unfair.

Chapter 8

Review

The letter "R" in **PROCEED**, stands for Review.

At this point you have:

- Learned about the three levels of the Response Pyramid™ and the importance of a *Level 3* response (the candidate's recall of a real experience that illustrates the presence or absence of a competency);

- Seen the "**SAFE**" model used to get details of a *Level 3* behavior-based example;

- Used the *Job Description Planner* format to create or edit a Job Description;

- Identified the Essential Job functions for a specific position;

- Listed Technical Skills plus key Work Habits for this position;

- Selected Work Habit questions and edited or modified them as necessary;

- Created new Work Habit questions;

- Authored Technical Skills questions.

This chapter will give you information to help you conduct a legal and fair interview.

After reading this chapter, audit your interview questions to verify their legality and fairness. If you have any doubts about legal issues, you should consult an attorney who specializes in labor relations or a human resources expert who has considerable experience in this area. After all the work you have done in preparing your interview questions, it seems almost unfair to burden you with the requirements of the law. Unfortunately, if your company has 15 or more employees, many of the requirements covered in this chapter apply directly to you. If you have less than 15 employees you may be subject to similar state laws that apply to employers with as few as four employees. If you are not subject to any of these laws, you have more freedom. However, it's not a bad idea to build an organization with the legal safeguards in place as a preventive measure. As your organization grows and you become subject to the various laws and regulations, you won't have to re-design your hiring system.

Several hundred federal laws and regulations are currently in place for employers to comply with. Plus, states have their own supplements and additions. At the federal level, companies often have to deal with the requirements of the Equal Employment Opportunities Commission (EEOC), the Immigration and Naturalization Service (INS), the Internal Revenue Service (IRS), the Department of Labor (DOL), the National Labor Relations Board (NLRB), and others.

The EEOC is the primary guardian of non-discrimination in employment. This agency has the duty to enforce the requirements of the Civil Rights Act of 1964 (as amended in 1991) and the Americans With Disabilities Act of 1990 including its enforcement guidance.

The Civil Rights Act of 1964, the ADA of 1990 (including the 1995 revision), plus many other regulations, prohibit discrimination on the basis of:

☐ Sex/Gender

☐ Pregnancy

☐ Age (if age 40 or older)

☐ Religion

☐ Color

☐ Race

☐ National Origin

☐ Citizenship

☐ Disability

☐ Military Service During the Vietnam-Era

Supporting equal employment opportunity is not only a legal requirement, it makes good business sense.

Your Legal IQ

Which of the following interview questions do you believe are, or may be, legal to ask under federal or state laws?

Sex/Gender related:

☐ This isn't a job for a woman, right?

☐ Are you comfortable traveling on overnight assignments with men?

☐ Is that a wedding ring on your finger?

☐ Is Wilson your maiden name?

☐ Are you married now or do you plan to get married soon?

☐ What are your arrangements for child care?

☐ Are you pregnant?

Age:

☐ What's your present age?

☐ When were you born?

☐ What year did you graduate from high school?

☐ When will you be old enough to receive Social Security retirement benefits?

☐ How old were you in the year 2000?

Religion:

☐ Are you Jewish?

☐ Why are you wearing that turban?

☐ How do you spend your Sundays?

☐ What church do you go to?

☐ Have you been "saved" or "born again"?

☐ Are you in the Knights of Columbus or any other religious group?

☐ Do your kids attend Sunday school?

☐ What religious holidays do you observe?

Color/Race:

☐ Are you Afro-American?

☐ What's your race?

National Origin/Citizenship:

☐ Is English your second language?

☐ Is that a Polish name?

☐ Where were you born?

☐ What country did your parents come from?

Military Service:

☐ Are you a Vietnam veteran?

☐ Did you serve in the military between 1964 and 1976?

Some of these questions may seem like innocent inquiries that represent a legitimate concern of yours. Unfortunately, every one of the above questions can be interpreted as a violation of a person's legal rights under federal or certain state laws.

Rather than asking questions like these, simply state a specific job requirement and ask the candidate if they are able to meet it. Example:

"This job requires fluency in Spanish. Do you meet this requirement?"

NOTE: Interviewers most often get themselves into hot water by asking illegal questions during the early stages of the interview while they are building rapport with the candidate or during those times when they are not following their structured interview process.

Disability

Because of its importance, I'll discuss the issue of disability in some detail. The regulations for employing people with disabilities will lead to major changes in your organization. The Americans With Disabilities Act of 1990 (ADA) and its revisions, bring the most sweeping changes to employment law in more than three decades. The Act describes in detail how you must accommodate disabled employees and prospective employees. It outlines requirements for how you interview job applicants and make your hiring decisions.

The regulations that make up the ADA fill about 350 pages of the Federal Register and cover a myriad of issues. Basically, the ADA prohibits discrimination against people who have, or are judged as having, a mental or physical impairment. The intent of Congress was to prevent discrimination of individuals with both obvious and hidden disabilities. Inquiries concerning the existence, nature, or severity of a disability are expressly forbidden by the legislation. The rules are not easy to interpret, and we are just now beginning to understand what they mean to employers. There are many vague provisions in the act which are best handled on a case-by-case basis. If you have questions about the ADA, talk to the appropriate people in your own organization and seek their advice (the Human Resources or Legal departments are your most likely starting points), consult an attorney who specializes in labor law, or contact the Equal Employment Opportunities Commission at (800) 669-4000.

Under ADA law, discrimination complaints are submitted to the Equal Employment Opportunities Commission (EEOC). The EEOC conducts an independent investigation and takes action as necessary to correct the situation. They also advise the person who initiated the complaint regarding their rights to sue an employer in federal court for compensatory and punitive damages.

As an employer, your best defense is to make a good-faith effort to comply with the law and treat job applicants and employees accordingly. This means your managers, supervisors, recruiters, interview team members, and human resources staff must know about the law in order to comply. Under the ADA, you may not make any pre-employment inquiries about disabilities, attendance, illness, or workers compensation history; on any job application, during interviews, or when checking background and references. Do not ask any of the following kinds of questions:

☐ Is there any health-related reason that would keep you from performing this kind of work?

☐ Have you had a major illness in the last five years?

☐ Do you have any physical defects, disabilities or impairments that would adversely affect your performance in this position?

☐ Have you ever been diagnosed or treated for the following illnesses or diseases: (List)?

☐ List the treatments you have received by a medical doctor or practitioner in the last three years.

☐ When were you last hospitalized?

☐ Have you ever seen a Psychologist, a Psychiatrist, or been treated for any mental condition?

☐ Are you taking any prescribed medications or drugs?

☐ Have you ever been treated for drug or alcohol abuse?

☐ How much alcohol do you consume on a daily, weekly, or monthly basis?

☐ Are you an alcoholic?

☐ Do you have AIDS, Tuberculosis, or any other contagious disease?

☐ Have you ever filed a workers' compensation insurance claim?

So now you say, "What can I ask about?" Keep in mind that the ADA is designed to get you to focus on a candidate's competencies and abilities, not their impairments. In addition to your structured interview questions, you may ask questions like these:

☐ Can you perform the essential functions of the job with or without an accommodation?

☐ How will you perform the task?

☐ Can you meet the job's work hours requirement (provided the requirement is a true representation of the job's work hours)?

Other questions you can ask (you should also ask these of your able-bodied candidates):

☐ Do you currently use illegal drugs?

☐ Have you been a casual user of illegal drugs in the past?

☐ Did you have any unauthorized absences from work last year?

☐ How many days were you absent from work last year?

You may also ask candidates to demonstrate how specific job functions would be performed even if every candidate for the job is not required to do so. If a candidate has a known disability that might interfere with this person's ability to perform a job function, you may ask the candidate how the function would be performed even if other applicants are not required to do so.

Reasonable Accommodation

A key principle in the ADA is reasonable accommodation. Reasonable accommodation is an adjustment the company must make to ensure an applicant is able to perform an Essential Job Function. The ADA requires employers to make reasonable accommodation for a qualified applicant or employee with a permanent disability so long as the accommodation does not cause undue business hardship or create a safety hazard to other employees. Undue business hardship means the accommodation would cause you to incur unreasonable expense, would be unsafe or disruptive to your business, or would alter the basic nature of your business.

Reasonable accommodation may include such things as: modifications to buildings and equipment; the addition of special devices such as voice recognition equipment for blind computer operators or paying for interpreters to convert spoken English into sign language for a deaf person; reassigning non-essential job duties to other workers; modifying break times or working hours; reserving parking spaces close to building entrances; or granting medical leaves to disabled workers who are temporarily unable to perform

Essential Job Functions due to their disability. Interpretations of what is reasonable accommodation change as challenges to the ADA are brought before the judicial system. When in doubt, consult an attorney or a human resources specialist who has current knowledge regarding recent court decisions.

According to the revised EEOC-published "Guidance on Pre-Employment Inquiries and Medical Examinations" (October, 1995), if an applicant voluntarily discloses the need for reasonable accommodation, or you believe the applicant may need an accommodation because of an obvious disability, you may ask questions about the type of accommodation needed. You may ask questions about reasonable accommodation only for those activities related to Essential Job Functions. However, if you ask a candidate about reasonable accommodation and the applicant is not hired, the EEOC may decide to investigate in order to determine if the reason for rejection was based on the candidate's need for accommodation.

Is it ever legal to fire a disabled worker?

In the case of *EEOC v. Kinney Shoe Corp.*, the employer hired a disabled worker who had epilepsy. The company hired the person knowing about the disability and provided reasonable accommodation. However, the employee suffered a number of seizures during his seven month employment which created a disruption of the company's business. The company fired the employee based on the facts surrounding the workers specific condition. The U. S. District Court in western Virginia upheld the firing and dismissed the case.

The ruling suggests that you can treat the performance of a disabled person just as you would any regular employee. You should give everyone an opportunity to be successful. If they fail, you can legally terminate them even if they are disabled. However, you can't fire an employee because their disability might have a negative effect on your customer relations. This argument was presented by the company, but rejected by the court.

Legitimate Reasons to Terminate an Employee

This discussion goes beyond the issue of hiring, but it should ease your concerns about hiring someone who is a member of a protected class.

Poor Performance. Generally, you can terminate an employee who is protected by law if you do two things:

☐ **Document performance.** Don't wait until you have accumulated a list of deficiencies before documenting them. Your documentation can be informal. A series of hand written notes in your "day-timer" or on plain sheets of paper, dated and filed in a folder, is sufficient. Along with the documentation, you should discuss instances of poor performance with the employee immediately upon becoming aware of the problem. Don't wait until you have a laundry-list of items and then dump them on the offender all at once.

☐ **Provide proper accommodation.** Other than for disability, you are not required to provide accommodation. However, the courts may look favorably upon employers who attempt to accommodate the special needs of their employees. You don't want to be portrayed as an ogre or a company that deprived a person of their livelihood because they were too old, pregnant, or conformed to the customs of their religion.

Downsizing or reorganization. In *Kathy Smith v. F.W. Morse & Company, Inc., 1996,* the employee was terminated while she was on maternity leave during a second round of downsizing. The trial court ruled that the termination was unrelated to her pregnancy and the decision was upheld by the U.S. Court of Appeals for the 1st Circuit.

Legitimate Reasons to Discriminate

There are legitimate reasons to discriminate in hiring when the requirements of the job make it impossible to do otherwise. This is called a bona fide occupational qualification (BFOQ) and is generally only available in the entertainment field. For example, if you were casting a movie about the early childhood of a black, Olympic decathlon champion, you don't have to hire a white woman in her forties to play the part.

If You Discriminate

Will the EEOC come after you? Unless they have a strong case against you, chances are, they won't. Their budget has been cut, forcing the agency to recently drop over 20,000 cases from its books. Its agents will most likely concentrate on the most flagrant violators. Individuals, however, can sue, and their attorneys must be paid by you if they win. Also, if you are a government contractor, you are subject to random audits.

Dealing with the legal aspects of hiring employees can seem like a formidable task to many interviewers. The "7 Step" system has been designed to minimize your legal risks and to help you create a legally defensible interview. If you use the system and stick to your prepared interview questions, you should be on safe ground.

Above all, there is a cardinal rule you should adhere to:

YOU MUST HAVE A LEGITIMATE BUSINESS REASON TO SUPPORT ANY QUESTION YOU ASK. DO NOT ASK QUESTIONS NOT DIRECTLY RELATED TO THE REQUIREMENTS OF THE JOB

If you need help, contact the following agencies:

● EEOC at (800) 669-4000 or (202) 663-4264;

● U.S. Department of Labor (202) 219-6666;

- ADA Information Line for documents, questions, and referrals (800) 514-0301, electronic bulletin board (202) 514-6193;

- Employer's Resource Center on the ADA and Workers With Psychiatric Disorders at (202) 408-9320;

- Disability & Business Technical Assistance Centers (800) 949-4232 (Your call automatically connects to the closest center).

As a business owner or manager you are obligated to become familiar with the law as it applies to your workplace. Knowing the law and building a fair, positive environment will help you to prevent costly employee lawsuits.

Interviewing and the Law — Time Table

I'll close this chapter with a brief summary of the legislation or court decisions that impact the hiring process. There are others, but you should at least develop a familiarity with those that follow. Dates shown refer to the initial year in which the legislation was first enacted. These laws have been modified and amended over the years to include new provisions.

1938: Fair Labor Standards Act

Establishes requirements for minimum wages and overtime pay. Applies to all employers engaged in interstate commerce. Birthplace of the terms "exempt" and "nonexempt" from overtime law. Burden of proof is on the employer to show an employee is exempt from overtime law. Exempted categories are executive, administrative, professional, and outside sales.

1964: Civil Rights Act (Title VII)

This landmark legislation was the most significant act passed by congress in the hundred years following the Civil War. Prohibits discrimination on the basis of sex, race, color, religion, and national origin.

1967: Age Discrimination Act

Prohibits discrimination on the basis of age between 40 and 70 years (the upper limit of 70 years was removed in 1978 with the passage of the Age Discrimination in Employment Act).

1970: EEOC Guidelines on Employee Selection

Introduced the requirement that employment tests must be job related. Adopted the American Psychological Association's *Standards for Educational and Psychological Tests* as the basis for employment test validation (Much confusion and uncertainty about the validity of employment tests has been the result of these EEOC guidelines).

1971: Griggs v. Duke Power Co.

Established the "business necessity" requirement for employment practices and laid the groundwork for the emergence of the principle of "adverse impact."

This case also reinforced the requirement that all pre-employment tests must be job related.

NOTE: "Adverse impact" is a statistical calculation to determine if your organization is using hiring practices which unintentionally discriminate against people who, by law, are protected against discrimination. The formula for this calculation appears in the Uniform Guidelines on Employee Selection Procedures.

1973: Vocational Rehabilitation Act

Established the requirement for employers to provide "reasonable accommodation" to applicants with disabilities. The accommodation includes building and grounds modifications for wheelchair access, special furniture and telephones, etc.

1975: Albermarle Paper Co. v. Moody

Created a barrier to aptitude testing in selection due to the many criticisms leveled against the validation method used.

1975: Pregnancy Discrimination Act

Prohibits discrimination against an applicant or employee because she is pregnant.

1978: Uniform Guidelines on Employment Selection Procedures

Allowed content, construct or criterion related validity as evidence of the validity of pre-employment tests (See discussion on page 147). Introduced the "adverse impact" calculation to determine if unintentional discrimination is present.

1986: Immigration Reform and Control Act

This legislation was designed to strengthen the anti-discrimination requirements of the Civil Rights Act of 1964 as it applies to national origin or citizenship. The act penalizes employers who discriminate and provides remedies for people who have been mistreated. The act also requires that employers check every employee's status for eligibility to work in the U.S. Employers comply by requiring new hires (whether they are U.S. citizens or non-citizens) to fill out Employment Eligibility Form I-9 within the first three days of employment.

1988: Employee Polygraph Protection Act

Private sector employers may not use lie detectors, voice print or related devices in the selection of employees. Some exceptions apply for security-related positions.

1990: Americans With Disabilities Act

Prohibits discrimination in employment against individuals with physical or mental disabilities who are qualified, with or without reasonable accommodation, to perform the essential functions of the job. This includes job application procedures, hiring, firing, advancement, compensation, training, and other terms, conditions, and privileges of employment. It applies to recruitment, advertising, tenure, layoff, leave, fringe benefits, and all other employment-related activities.

1991: Civil Rights Act

Makes U.S. discrimination laws applicable to U.S. nationals working for U.S. companies anywhere in the world.

1993: Family Medical Leave Act

Comprehensive legislation that covers family and medical leaves for employees of companies that employ 50 or more workers for 20 or more workweeks in the current or preceding calendar year. The FMLA provides up to 12 weeks of unpaid leave for serious health problems, childbirth, adoption, placement of a foster child, or to care for a child, spouse, or parent with a serious health condition. Leave may be taken on an intermittent or reduced work hours basis. Employers must continue group health insurance benefits to an employee during the leave.

> **To do:**
> Review the questions you have developed and eliminate or re-write those that are discriminatory. Refer to the guidelines listed below as you conduct your review.

Remove or re-write interview questions that:

☐ Inquire about knowledge, skills, or abilities NOT required of ALL candidates BEFORE employment;

☐ Cannot be directly linked to Essential Job Functions;

☐ Refer directly or indirectly to race, color, national origin, sex/gender, religion, age. marital status, child care, transportation, mental or physical disabilities, membership in clubs, arrest records;

☐ Inquire about personal habits, finances, and politics, unless you can demonstrate a direct link to job requirements;

☐ Inquire about worker's compensation history or current use of prescription drugs.

Chapter 9

Organize

Up to this point, you have created a series of interview questions, each linked to a Work Habit or a Technical Skill. These Work Habits and Technical Skills are, in turn, linked to Essential Job Functions. You have reviewed your questions for legality and fairness and now you are ready to complete the final step before you begin your interviews. You will need to consider:

- The page layout for your structured interview questions;

- The type of interview — *Individual, Sequential Interviews, Panel Interviews*, or a combination;

- Who will be conducting interviews;

- How to assign questions to interviewers;

- How you will schedule interviews;

- How you will train other interviewers;

- Whether to supplement your interviews with tests.

Page Layout

The most useful page layout:

☐ Has the definition of the Work Habit or Technical Skill printed at the top of each page for easy reference;

☐ Contains no more than two interview questions per page with plenty of room to take notes;

☐ Includes an answer key beneath each technical question that has a correct answer.

Print the Definition at the Top of Each Page

The definition of a Work Habit or Technical Skill is the foundation for your interview questions. If you print the definition at the top of each page, you will be constantly reminded to seek information that relates to the definition. It also helps keep your questions organized. Remember when you were busy writing those questions and I said you will need at least two questions per interviewer for each competency? With two questions per page, all you do is hand a different page to each interviewer. You now have created a process where each interviewer has a unique set of questions to ask the job candidate. Furthermore, since no two interviewers will ask the same questions, the candidate cannot practice his or her answers and make them sound better in subsequent interviews. Plus, you build a much richer data base of information to consult when it's time to evaluate a candidate's competencies.

How to Create a New Question From the Definition.

Occasionally, you will want more information about a job candidate's competency than you get from just two questions. If this happens, you can create a new question in real-time, based on the definition of the competency that appears at the top of the page.

Here's what to do:

☐ Read the definition at the top of the page;

☐ Select an area of the definition that relates to the information you need;

☐ Ask an open-ended question that requires the candidate to describe an appropriate past experience.

Example:

Recently I interviewed a candidate for a position as a Customer Service Representative for a software company. As I listened to her describe her experiences, I became concerned about her treatment of customers after the immediate problem was addressed.

The definition of Customer Satisfaction is: "Ability to build productive relationships with internal or external customers in order to build customer loyalty and business success."

As I read the definition of Customer Satisfaction, I zeroed in on the words "build customer loyalty". I then asked: "What have you done with a customer to build loyalty or repeat business?" Her answer confirmed that she did very little follow up and was not concerned about determining if the customer was fully satisfied or felt comfortable in calling on her for help with future problems.

A Special Option. You have a set of questions to refer to as you conduct your interview, so why not give this same advantage to your candidate? Some people find it easier to receive information by listening. Others prefer to read the printed word. To accommodate both styles, print a copy of each question on a 4x6 inch index card. As you ask a candidate the question, hand the index card to the person. Let them read the question and refer to it as they respond. It will help them maintain focus and you are more likely to get a response that is richer in detail and more complete than you would by just asking the question itself. Of course, you will want to retrieve the card once the candidate has given you the example.

Type of Interview — Individual, Sequential or Panel

Individual interviews. If you are the only person interviewing candidates you will be limited to gathering as much data as you can from a single interview. A small company often finds itself in this situation. The owner may prefer to personally conduct all the interviews. Sometimes a person other than the owner is given the task. Since this interviewer is limited to one data point, the individual interview is exposed to the probability of increased error. Here's what you can do to minimize errors if this is your situation:

☐ Do a careful and complete *Preparation* step;

☐ Prepare and ask more than two questions about each competency;

☐ Ask every prepared question to every candidate;

☐ Use tests to supplement your interviews (See pages 145-151);

☐ Do a thorough evaluation of the candidate's competencies (as described in Chapter 12);

☐ Check references carefully and completely;

☐ Contract with an agency to complete a background check before you make an offer;

☐ When you make a job offer to a candidate, indicate they are being hired for an "introductory" period during which time they may be terminated with or without cause.

Sequential interviews involve a series of one-on-one interviews where the candidate is passed from interviewer to interviewer. Sequential interviews have the advantage of providing multiple sources of information to help you make a high quality hiring decision. Let's face it, each of us has our own interviewing style. Some people find it easier than others to establish rapport with a candidate who has a social style different from their own. We each have varying abilities to communicate and to effectively gather information during the interview. If we are interviewing a candidate for technical ability, some of us may be more up to date on the technology than others. With multiple data points, we can more accurately evaluate a candidate's skills by taking advantage of each interviewer's strengths while mitigating their shortcomings.

For Sequential interviews, assign each interviewer a series of questions to ask. If you can, it's best to assign **only** Technical Skill questions to one or two interviewers and assign **only** Work Habit questions to one or two other interviewers.

Work Habit Interviewers. Your Work Habit interviewers should have two questions for each of the six to eight Work Habits that make up the job. If you assign questions in this manner, you will have a much larger data base of information to tap when you evaluate the match between a job candidate's skills and the requirements of the job.

Technical Skill interviewers. There are two basic options for these interviewers. One option is to assign two or more questions for each Technical Skill to each interviewer in order to cover a broad range of skills. A second option is to group your technical questions according to the area of expertise for which they have been created. Then assign each group of questions to the interviewer who has the most in-depth technical knowledge for that area.

Panel interviews are conducted by a team composed of two to five members. These interviews are very effective when properly conducted. It takes some planning to realize the benefits from this type of interview. I'm sure you have either talked to people who have had some awful experiences being interviewed by a panel or have had some of these experiences yourself. A properly managed panel interview is not an inquisition or an interrogation. It's a time-efficient method for gathering competency-based information about a job candidate's skills. It gives interviewers an opportunity to play off each other's questions. Panel members have the advantage of observing the interaction between the candidate and other interviewers along with a little extra time to take notes. Also, everyone on the interview panel hears the same information at the same time. Finally, panel interviews are often more effective than sequential interviews at predicting future job success.

Recommendations For Conducting Panel Interviews

Appoint a leader for the panel. The interview panel leader:

- Introduces the candidate to each member of the interviewing panel;

- Insures that all panel members are given an opportunity to ask questions;

- Manages interactions between interviewers and the candidate;

- Manages time;

- Insures that the interview is properly documented;

- Closes the interview;

- Provides a single point of interface for panel members and the candidate;

- Prepares the candidate for the interview;

- Selects a non-threatening environment for the interview;

- Assigns responsibility to one person to complete necessary follow-up.

Why not try a mixture? Conduct two or three sequential interviews either followed or preceded by a panel interview. In this way, your candidates will have an opportunity to see a half-dozen or more people in a single day.

Most organizations "over-kill" when it comes to interviewing candidates. As a rule, three or four interviewers can gather enough data to evaluate a candidate's skills. If candidates are going to interview with more than four people, let the other interviewers handle matters such as "selling" the organization, explaining benefits, work rules, policies and conditions, organization structure, products, markets, etc., and answering candidate's questions.

Selecting and Training Interviewers

A good choice for the interviewing team would be:

☐ One or two technical content experts;

☐ One or two members of management;

☐ One or two peers.

Interviewers asking questions about Technical Skills or Work Habits should have expert knowledge about the job the candidate is interviewing for. The hiring manager, a person doing the same job, and a next level manager would also be good choices for the interview team.

Train your interviewers in the "7 Step" process. Work with them to insure that they know how to gain a *Level 3* behavior-based example and can probe for details.

As stated in the *Special Note* at the beginning of Chapter 5, involve your interview team in the skills analysis and let them help you draft interview questions.

Scheduling

Most interviews last from between 45 minutes to 1 hour and 30 minutes depending on the:

- Level and complexity of the job;

- Preparation and skill of the interviewer;

- Candidate's communication skills and depth of experience.

Each interviewer will most likely have from 12 to 24 questions to ask the job candidate. My experience indicates it takes from two to four minutes to ask a behavior-based question, listen to the candidate's response, and probe for details. Of course you will be doing other things in addition to asking questions, so you can see why a well conducted interview will last an hour or more.

When you schedule interviews, remember to add a 20 to 30 minute block of time immediately following each interview in order to:

- Clean up your notes;

- Evaluate the candidate's skills;

- Decide on the next step for this candidate;

- Prepare for your next interview.

A Final Note on Scheduling Interviews

Many organizations unintentionally burn candidates out by scheduling too many interviews for them in a single day. Interviews are stressful experiences for most candidates and consume a good deal of physical and mental energy.

To make your interviews productive, two or three skill assessment interviews in a single day are plenty. If you want to add an information interview to the schedule, that's fine. This way you could schedule two interviews in the morning and one or two in the afternoon.

Interviewing a candidate during a meal presents the candidate with some special issues: talking and eating at the same time; trying to listen to the interviewer(s) over background noise; and dealing with interruptions. Use meals as an opportunity to build greater rapport with the candidate, give them information about your organization and the job, and, if required by the job, observe their social skills.

Pre Employment Testing

When we think of testing, what comes to mind is the paper and pencil variety many of us have been exposed to in the past. Did you know, according to the law, the entire interviewing process from initial screening to reference checking can be construed to be a test? That's why it's important for you to use a system that helps create structured interviews directly tied to the requirements of the job.

Pre-employment testing remains a controversial issue. For employers, testing can give them important information and cut the cost of hiring and training for new employees. Properly done, testing can help organizations match the candidate's skills to the requirements of the job. The downside is that testing can also screen out qualified candidates, discriminate against protected classes, and add to the cost of hiring in the long run. If a candidate is offended by your tests, they may take you to court. You could be charged with discrimination or even invasion of privacy. In the case of *Soroka v. Dayton Hudson Corp.,* Dayton Hudson of California, settled out of court for $2,000,000. The candidate objected to the company's use of test questions which probed sexual, medical, and religious beliefs and practices.

Testing was popular in the 1960's and was on the decline during the 1980's. In this first decade of the new millennium testing is once again on the rise. A survey sponsored by the Olsten Corporation indicated that more than 60% of the companies in their sample of 577 have, or are considering, implementing skills testing as a condition of employment. An additional 29% say they have, or are considering implementing personality and/or aptitude testing.

Reliability and Validity in Pre-employment testing. There are two measures you should pay close attention to if you plan to supplement your interviews with tests: reliability and validity. *Reliability* refers to the consistency of measurement. Are the results of the test repeatable? If I give you a test today and sometime in the future, can I be assured the results will be the same, provided nothing the test measures has changed? If I can, the test has high reliability. *Validity* is concerned with two different questions: does the test measure what it claims to measure (this is called *Content* validity)? For hiring decisions though, I want to know if a test will actually predict who will succeed or fail on the job (this is known as *Criterion* validity). Those tests that do measure what they say they measure and also predict success on the job, have high *Content* and *Criterion* validity.

The challenge in testing is finding valid instruments that do not discriminate against those groups protected by law. Concerns about validity have prompted some companies to adopt "race norming" where scores are adjusted so that proportionate numbers of each racial and ethnic group will pass a test. Our advice: do not use different cutoff scores or adjust scores for people of different races, color, gender, religion, national origin or citizenship.

There are over 1,400 tests on the market today. Firms such as the Consulting Psychologists Press in Palo Alto, California, and The Psychological Corporation in San Antonio, Texas, publish a variety of standardized tests. *The Mental Measurements Yearbook,* which can be found in many public libraries, provides descriptions and reviews of most tests available today.

Types of tests that are most popular:

Skills — related to job content.

Example: The *Common Metric Questionnaire (CMQ)* which uses an instrument to help you complete a job skills analysis. It offers a more exhaustive process than the one outlined in Chapters 5-7 to identify competencies required to do a job. The CMQ is not directly linked to a job description but can be used to produce a job description and identify Essential Job Functions.

Personality assessment — to measure traits such as emotional stability, introversion, etc.

Example: The *California Psychological Inventory.* Measures characteristics such as independence, dominance, tolerance, social presence, self-control, empathy, and creativity.

Achievement — to ascertain the degree of knowledge in a particular field.

Example: *Adult Basic Learning Examination (ABLE)* is made up of a battery of independent subject-specific sub tests that provide a reliable measure of adult educational achievement.

Aptitude — to determine capabilities, comprehension, interests and teachability.

Example: The *Guilford-Zimmerman Aptitude Survey* which measures six different areas of aptitude: verbal comprehension, general reasoning, numerical operations, perceptual speed, and spatial visualization. Any of these six areas can be tested independently, or combined to measure the most important abilities for a given job.

Honesty tests — to screen out dishonest workers.

Example: *Reid Report.* Measures attitudes about honesty, theft, safety, policies, rules and regulations, etc.

Intelligence tests — to determine intellectual capability.

Example: The *Wechsler Adult Intelligence Scale - Revised (WAIS-R)* produces IQ (Intelligence Quotient) scores for adults. This is one of the most widely used adult IQ tests.

If your company is considering using some of these commercially available tests, do so with professional guidance. You should also be aware, according to the *Uniform Guidelines on Employee Selection Procedures*, you have the responsibility to make sure any test you adopt is being used appropriately by your organization.

NOTE: The examples of tests I have cited are not recommendations, but merely convenient examples.

Testing and the "Four-Fifths" rule

To determine if you are discriminating against a protected class in your testing, keep data on who passes and who fails. If the ratio of the percentage of those passing the test for the protected group as compared to those passing the test who are members of the majority is less than 4/5, you are creating adverse impact according to the law.

Example:

Percent passing from the protected group: 50%

Percent passing from the majority group: 75%

Ratio = .50/.75 = .667 or 67%

Four-fifths = 4/5 = .8 or 80%.

Therefore, this test does not meet requirements of the "Four-Fifths" rule and is not in compliance with the law.

The Equal Employment Opportunities Commission (EEOC) has established guidelines to make testing fair and legal when used as a selection device along with job-related interviews and reference checks. In other words, *tests should not be the only basis upon which a hiring decision is made.* For answers to legal questions regarding testing, contact the EEOC at (800) 669-4000.

Three principal documents are used as guidelines to set up and validate selection test programs.

The first document is the *Uniform Guidelines on Employee Selection Procedures* (1978) contains the requirements of the U.S. Civil Service Commission, the Department of Justice, the Equal Employment Opportunity Commission, and the Department of labor. This is probably the most important reference document for creating and administering legally defensible employment tests.

The others are: *Standards for Educational and Psychological Tests* available from the American Psychological Association, Hyattsville, Maryland; and *Principles for the Validation and Use of Personnel Selection Procedures* available from the Society for Industrial and Organizational Psychology, Arlington Heights, Illinois.

Remember: TESTS MUST BE VALID AND DIRECTLY RELATED TO THE SKILLS NEEDED FOR THE JOB. If a test does not meet these requirements, it should not be used as part of your selection process.

Chapter 10

Conduct — Part I

This is what you've been waiting for. You've finally arrived. The candidate is waiting at the door. You're ready to conduct your behavior-based interview. Or are you?

Have you reviewed the applicant's résumé? If not, let's take a few minutes to discuss this often misunderstood document. Unfortunately, the word "résumé" to many employers and candidates alike, has become synonymous with "marketing piece." Rather than looking for useful information, we begin judging the résumé for it's advertising qualities. If you have read other "how to hire" books, they often encourage you to focus on the shortcomings of a résumé rather than extracting the beneficial information it contains. Fortunately, for some applicants, many companies now use scanners to extract information from résumés and they use computers to match applicant information to job requirements.

The résumé can be a dangerous tool in the wrong hands. That is, information on the résumé may cause a person to pre-judge a candidate before the evidence is in. For this reason, regard the résumé as a starting point, a place to begin an honest search for data to help you determine if a candidate has the knowledge, skills, and experience to do the job. Resist the temptation to judge a résumé good or bad and extend this judgment to the candidate as well.

> **To do:**
> Review a résumé submitted by a job applicant with help from the guidelines below.

☐ Dig out the Job Description or your *Job Description Planner* information for this position. Retrieve the interview questions for Technical Skills.

Search the résumé for the following information:

☐ Employment Objective — Is an objective listed and does it seem consistent with the position applied for?

☐ Experience — Look for evidence of what this person has accomplished, not just where they have worked or what job titles they had.

What information has the applicant provided that will help you evaluate their technical skills?

Do you need to clarify or question anything in the candidate's description of their work experience?

☐ Education — Does the education listed meet the minimum requirement for the job?

What other information do you need about the applicant's educational background?

☐ Training — Has this person participated in any training programs that satisfy a technical job requirement?

☐ Other — Are there gaps in the candidate's work history that need clarification?

Does the length of employment for any job need explanation?

Does this position seem like a logical next step for this person?

Review any other helpful information such as memberships in professional associations or licenses and certificates earned.

Sources of Error in the Interview

Okay. Now you're ready to go, right? Well, not quite. There's just one more little item. Before you begin your interview, you should be aware of a few "land mines" that may be in your path. I'm talking about some of the factors that create errors in the interview. To be forewarned is to be forearmed. So, let's take a look.

Interviewer Bias

Every interviewer is biased! When I refer to bias, what I mean is, "A unique point of view based on a person's past experiences." We're not talking about prejudice here, but rather the perspective one has when interacting with another person. Each of us has our own cultural heritage, age group, differing amounts of education, religious background, etc. These factors enable us to view people in our own unique way. It sometimes causes us to see what we want to see and not what is really there.

What can be done to minimize interviewer bias?

First, if you are made aware of bias, pay attention to those things that might inappropriately influence your decisions or cause you to make erroneous assumptions. Once you are aware of this type of error, you have the power to avoid it.

Another way to minimize bias is to use more than one interviewer in order to "see" the candidate from various points of view.

Stereotyping

Stereotypes are pre-conceived ideas about what characteristics are present in members of a certain group. Stereotypes are applied to individuals who are members of the group without consideration of individual differences. For example, males have been stereotyped as "good managers" while females have been stereotyped as "good administrative assistants." Interviewers often share a stereotype about a "good applicant" which insures they agree. Agreement however, does not guarantee accuracy.

When you hold a stereotypical view of someone, you are prone to judge that person—often in a negative way. Your goal in the interview is to move beyond the natural tendency to stereotype someone and ask questions designed to give you information about a candidate's job related skills.

Cloning Error

How often have you met someone who worked for an organization you once worked for, or who attended the same school you did? Isn't it natural to attribute your good qualities to that person because they had an affiliation with an organization you were once part of? This is called "cloning" or "mirror imaging."

Physical Appearance

Extensive research has been done on the impact of attractiveness on interview ratings. While the results have been mixed, earlier studies have indicated being physically attractive is a distinct advantage. More recent studies minimize the impact of physical attractiveness. More importantly, as an interviewer, you should be aware if a candidate's physical appearance triggers positive or negative feelings in you.

If a certain physical appearance is not a bona fide requirement for the job based on business necessity, then you should not allow it to impact your hiring decision.

Premature Decision Making

Each of us has a preferred decision style. Some of us prefer to make snap judgments based on first impressions while others want to delay decisions until every shred of information is in. Research shows that, in interview situations, many of us will make snap judgments about a candidate. Interestingly enough, this includes many people who would otherwise wait for more data before making a decision. Most interviewers will decide whether or not to hire a candidate during the first four to nine minutes of the interview. The best remedy for this problem is to withhold judgment until the interview is over and then examine the data you have gathered in light of the skills required for the job.

Personal Theories

Many interviewers employ personal theories in an attempt to separate those who will succeed on the job from those who will fail. They use their theories as a way to eliminate candidates based on subjective criteria. For example, a well known founder of a department store chain would take potential employees to lunch. If the candidate salted their food before tasting it, they were eliminated based on the assumption this behavior demonstrated a lack of intelligence. Another business owner I knew would only hire people who read his company's annual report before coming to the interview. His theory – "These are the kind of motivated, self starters this company needs" (his company has since filed for protection under bankruptcy law).

Inappropriate Setting

Consider the physical setting where you conduct interview. Hotel lobbies and airports are usually poor choices for holding interviews, as are cafeterias and shop floors. Distractions and noise will inhibit the ability of the candidate to concentrate and will keep you from giving the interview the attention it needs. Make arrangements for conducting your interview in a comfortable setting, free of interruptions. Please put your pager away or turn it off during the interview. If you interview in your office or work space, forward your telephone so it won't disrupt the discussion.

Taking the candidate to lunch or supper

What could be wrong with this? When you identified the Essential Job Functions and the skills needed to perform these functions, did you list table manners? If not, there is no need to evaluate them. Let someone who is not a member of the interviewing team take the candidate to lunch or supper. Here's a personal experience to illustrate how problematic a meal can be:

I applied for my first job as an engineer with an electronics company in "Silicon Valley". After two exhausting days of back-to-back interviews, I was invited to dinner at the close of the second day. My host was the Engineering Division, Vice President. Let me tell you, I was excited and impressed. Here I was, fresh from college and I was invited to dine with a vice president! I met him at his office at six o'clock in the evening. He took me to one of those "sophisticated" restaurants (the ones with linen tablecloths, real china, etc.) in Palo Alto. The vice president had a martini. I ordered milk (I know...milk!). We talked for awhile and I felt I was doing okay, but I was really worn out.

The soup was served at seven o'clock. I picked up the pepper shaker to spice up my soup. Suddenly, I lost my grip on the shaker and it landed hard in my soup bowl. If that wasn't embarrassing enough, a big blob of cream of mushroom soup left my bowl as if it had wings. It landed on the vice president's tie and I think some of it hit the lapel of his expensive jacket. I proceeded to make the situation worse by trying to wipe it off.

The tie must have been his favorite because I was notified the next day that it might be wise for me to focus my job search elsewhere.

I learned three things from that experience: green ties and cream of mushroom soup are not very compatible; keep your hands in your lap when you dine with a prospective employer; meals often do not provide the most appropriate setting for interviews!

Let's Get Started

Before the Candidate Arrives:

☐ Make arrangements to prevent interruptions during the interview;

☐ Check the environment — is it comfortable and professional looking;

☐ Gather any materials you want to give the candidate (e.g. annual report, company brochure, press articles, product literature, etc.);

☐ Look over your structured interview questions;

☐ Take a final look at the candidate's résumé and other relevant information you may have;

☐ Take careful note of the candidate's name;

☐ Find out what the candidate is scheduled to do following the interview.

Open the Interview

> NOTE: See Appendix D, pages 291-293 for an Interview Checklist you can reproduce and use during your interviews.

Greet the Candidate and Build Rapport. The purpose of rapport building is to put candidates at ease. After all, interviewing is a stressful experience for most people. It's not something they do all the time. They come to talk with you about their competencies with the hope that they accurately and effectively portray their skills and abilities. Your job as an interviewer is to help them give you good data. So, you need to put candidates at ease and assure them you will take full responsibility for getting high quality information from them.

Here's how it might look:

You (Standing and smiling)— "Susan, I'm pleased that you were able to join us today.

Susan — "Thank you, so am I"

You — "I've been looking forward to our talk together. Please have a seat." (you both sit) Would you like a cup of coffee, water, a soda?"

Susan — "No thank you. I'm fine."

You — "Susan, as you know, you're here to interview for the position of technical writer. In this position, you'll be reporting to Wayne Spencer. I supervise a group like Wayne's in the Telecom Division and I'm helping him interview job candidates. I want to assure you my role is to help you give me good information about your skills. With this information we'll be in a better position to decide how well your skills meet the requirements of the job."

Susan — "Okay"

You — " Is there anything else you need before we begin?"

Susan — "No, I don't think so."

BEHIND THE SCENE

This is what you did that was effective:

☐ Greeted Susan by her first name and used it more than once;

☐ Indicated you are looking forward to the interview;

☐ Invited her to sit down and offered her a refreshment;

☐ Reminded her of the job she was interviewing for;

☐ Described your position and its relationship to the job;

☐ Clarified your role and assured her you are the one responsible for conducting a successful interview;

☐ Checked with Susan for readiness to move to the next step.

Review the Schedule

You — "Okay, let me review your schedule for today so you know exactly what's happening. Here's a copy of your schedule with the interviewers' names, times, and locations (you hand her a copy). Our interview will last until about ten o'clock or so. I'll take you over to our break room and we can spend a few minutes there before your next interview. It looks like you'll be meeting with Mary Fuller at ten thirty and I'll escort you to her area. She'll be with you through lunch. Mary knows all the good eating spots in the area, so I think you're in for a treat at lunch time. After lunch, you'll have an opportunity to meet with Wayne for as long as necessary. Do you have any questions about the schedule?"

Susan — "I thought I was going to talk with Pat Neuman today."

You — "Well, I'll check this out for you, but I think Pat is off-site today. We'll certainly make sure the two of you have a chance to get together. Let me get Alicia (Susan's Human Resources contact) working on this (you write yourself a reminder)."

BEHIND THE SCENE

This is what you did that was effective:

☐ Gave Susan a copy of the schedule;

☐ Reviewed times so Susan has a sense of the overall schedule;

☐ Let her know someone would be with her at all times to escort her from place to place;

☐ Let her know a break was coming where she could relax and freshen up if necessary;

☐ Explained arrangements for lunch;

☐ Gave her a chance to ask questions;

☐ Took responsibility to get Human Resources to reschedule her interview with Pat Neuman.

Review the Agenda for the Interview

Give the candidate a blueprint so they have an understanding of where you are going.

You — "Susan, I'm going to be asking you a series of questions to highlight your background and your skills. First we'll briefly cover your work history. Next we'll take a look at the duties and responsibilities of your current job. Following this, I'm going to ask you some specific questions about your work experience. Then, I'll tell you a little bit about how Wayne's department works with my department and about some of the other people you'll work with. I'll also be happy to answer any questions about our company and how we're organized."

BEHIND THE SCENE

This is what you did that was effective:

□ Outlined step-by-step the flow of this interview;

□ Identified yourself as a "Technical Skills" interviewer;

□ Let Susan know that she will have an opportunity to ask questions;

□ Created an opening to sell your company to her.

Explain That You Will be Taking Notes.

You — "Susan, you probably noticed I have a stack of papers in front of me. Well, I have to confess, these are the questions I'm going to ask you. But, since I don't have a perfect memory, I'm going to be taking notes as we go though these questions. This also means I won't be able to maintain eye contact with you all the time. I hope this won't bother you. I need to look down to write my notes so I don't scribble. I can assure you even though I'm not looking up, I'm still listening. So, you just keep right on talking, okay?"

Susan — "Okay. Thanks for the warning."

You — "By-the-way. After your interview, if you'd like to see my notes, that's fine with me."

BEHIND THE SCENE

This is what you did that was effective:

☐ Let Susan know you will be using prepared questions (a structured interview process);

☐ Told her you would be taking notes;

☐ Gave yourself permission to break eye contact to take notes;

☐ Minimized threat by letting her know there would be nothing in your notes she could not see.

Clarify or Add Information to the Résumé as Necessary.

Remember before the interview when you reviewed Susan's résumé? If you need clarification, this is the time to ask. However, keep your questions legal! Don't ask if "Waysynzki" (Susan's last name) is Polish. Get the information you need to fill in gaps or further your understanding of information she presented in her résumé.

You — "Susan, before we get down to specifics, I have a question about your résumé. It says here you worked for the Rochester Electronics Corporation from 1994 to 1997. When exactly did you leave Rochester?"

Susan — "I left in February."

You — "Okay. Then you say you began work at Vertex in June."

Susan — "I can explain. My mother, she's widowed and was just diagnosed with cancer. She took it very hard and since she had no one else, I felt it was important for me to be with her. I asked Rochester if I could take a leave of absence. Unfortunately they were laying off at the time and wouldn't agree, so I had to quit."

You — "I'm sorry about that. Thank you for filling in the gap. One other item — you mentioned you received a community service award. What was that about?"

Susan — "Believe it or not, it was related to my mom's illness. I got involved in our local hospital's volunteer program. I just spent time visiting terminally ill patients. Before I knew it, I was given the job of coordinating all the volunteers. We started a series of workshops for the patients and it just took off. We had almost every patient involved in one way or another. The chamber of commerce heard about it and I guess they decided we were making some sort of unique contribution. I'll have to say..."

You — (interrupting) "That's very interesting, and commendable. But now I'd like to turn our attention to your job at Vertex."

BEHIND THE SCENE

This is what you did that was effective:

☐ Avoided illegal questions;

☐ Filled in a gap in her employment history;

☐ Tactfully acknowledged her reason for leaving Rochester;

☐ Built greater rapport and gained some additional information by asking about her community service award;

☐ Tactfully interrupted her story to bring the interview back to the mainstream.

Begin With a Review of the Duties and Responsibilities for the Candidate's Current or Last Job.

This helps you by giving you a "jumping-off" place. It also helps tie the questions you are going to ask to the candidate's real-world experience. Even if this information is on the résumé, this is a painless way to begin the interview.

You — "Susan, tell me about the duties and responsibilities of your last job."

Susan — "Okay. I was responsible for all of the documentation for our software manuals. These manuals are used for internal purposes, but since we have over eight thousand employees, they had to be well done. I personally wrote about twenty percent of the content for our last three manuals. Of course, I wasn't the content expert, so I had to interview a lot of people."

You — "You said something I would like more information about. You said you wrote twenty percent of the content. Who wrote the rest?"

Susan — "We actually wrote as a team. There were four other writers and we divided the writing more-or-less equally."

You — "How did you bring all of this information together?"

Susan — "We did it in a series of meetings. Our senior writer would bring us together and we would review the outline of what each person was responsible for. Then she would ask each of us to read a sample of our work to insure that we were following her style and editorial guidelines."

You — "How well did that system work?"

Susan — "To tell you the truth, I was pretty skeptical at first, but it worked very well! I was always used to giving my work to a senior editor, then spending a lot of time in re-write. I'll bet we shaved about thirty percent off the production time. You know, I'm curious to see if that system would work here."

You — "Yes, I certainly hope you have an opportunity to try it."

BEHIND THE SCENE

This is what you did that was effective:

☐ Uncovered some detailed information about her role as a team member you would have missed if you hadn't asked for it;

☐ Confirmed she was able to use interviews as a way to gather content information;

☐ Found out she was willing to try a new method of writing;

☐ Learned she worked collaboratively as part of a team;

Train the Candidate to Respond With Behavior-Based Examples.

This is the time to explain the behavior-based system to the candidate. You should cover the Response Pyramid™ and details of a *Level 3* response. This will save you a lot of time and will speed up the learning process for the candidate.

You — "Susan, some of the questions I'm going to ask are purely technical in nature and will help me to gauge the depth of your technical knowledge. Other questions will require that you recall some very specific events in your work history. I'll ask you to describe these situations to me in detail. Let me show you exactly what I want" (you hand Susan a sheet of paper with the Response Pyramid™ on it). "When I ask someone to tell me about a past experience, I often get descriptions like: 'I'm a great organizer' or 'I'm a leader'(you point to *Level 1*). This doesn't give me any useful information about their skills. Sometimes they say, 'I've always been able to solve tough problems or here's what I would do if I came across that situation' (you point to *Level 2*). Once again, I don't get useful information. What I'm really after is a detailed description about a real event, giving me names, dates, times, numbers, locations, and the like (you point to *Level 3*). It's sort of like an iceberg. All the good information is below the surface. I've got a neat little recipe I use to help you give me the kind of information I need (you turn the paper over and show Susan the model). Here it is. First, I'll ask you to tell me about the **S**etting or background. Then I'll ask you to describe what **A**ctions you and others took. I'll finish by asking you about the **F**inal outcome and get your **E**valuation of the outcome.

BEHIND THE SCENE

This is what you did that was effective:

☐ Let her know that some, but not all questions would be behavior-based;

☐ Gave her a verbal and visual description of the Response Pyramid™ including some examples;

☐ Emphasized the need to get a *Level 3* response;

☐ Verbally and visually reviewed your data gathering model;

☐ Gave Susan an aid she could refer to (paper with the description of your model).

Ask Your Prepared Questions.

Start by asking your pre-written questions. Even though you should read your questions exactly as they are written, you have several choices regarding the sequencing of these questions.

Use a Linear Sequence. To conduct a linear interview, start with the first question on the first page of your interview and ask each question in the order in which they appear in your interview. If your goal is consistency, this is the sequence to use.

Use Logic Links. For example, If you are asking a question about *Adaptability* and the candidate's answer causes you to wonder about *Vigilance*, it makes sense to jump to a prepared question on *Vigilance*. When the candidate has answered your question, either return to your questions about *Adaptability* or jump to another competency. When you've finished your Logic Links, go back to the beginning of your interview and pick up the questions you missed. Keep in mind your goal is to get enough data to evaluate the candidate's skills.

Use Modified Logic Links. Pick a competency to explore. Ask all the questions you have prepared for that competency. Then, decide what competency is the most logical choice to jump to next. Jump to the selected competency and ask all the questions for that one. Then repeat the process until you have covered all competencies that make up your structured interview.

Probe for Additional Information as You Ask Your Questions

Clarify — Ask for more information or elaboration. Examples: "Tell me more about it", "Please explain what you mean by ..." Inquire about who, what, where, when, why, and how.

Reflect — Express what you believe is the candidate's intended meaning associated with their statement.

Summarize — Restate your understanding of the main points covered by the candidate's answer or example.

Confirm — Help the candidate tie the answer to the skill you are asking about. Example: "How does this relate to your leadership skills or how does this illustrate your ability to troubleshoot an electrical problem?"

Expand — Pursue a new line of thought based on the candidate's response. Explore briefly, then return to the main theme of your question.

Persist — Repeat or rephrase the question, or use silence as a form of pressure to get a response. Don't quit until you have the data you need. If you don't understand something, ASK!

Make Your Interview A Sure-Fire Success

Here are some other things you can do to guarantee your interview will be productive and of high quality:

Document the Interview

Since behavior-based employment interviewing is data-driven, you need a reliable source of information in order to make a meaningful hiring decision. Your notes provide the source.

Note taking during an interview is one of the most difficult tasks you will undertake. The following guidelines will help ease this burden.

☐ Remember to include no more than two questions on each page of your structured interview form (You need plenty of room for notes).

☐ Write the name of the skill and its definition at the top of each page.

☐ Let the candidate know you will be taking notes during the interview and get their agreement to do so.

☐ Keep your notes brief. Record a few facts about the SETTING, the ACTIONS, the FINAL OUTCOME and EVALUATION. These are adequate to refresh your memory about a specific event.

☐ Don't include judgments or interpretations in your notes or write them on the candidate's résumé.

Use Silence to Build Pressure

When you ask a candidate for a behavior-based example of past experience, the candidate will break eye contact with you and look away. This is your signal to remain silent in order to give the candidate time to think. If you rescue the candidate or otherwise break the silence, you will only interrupt the candidate's train of thought.

Resist the temptation to fill silence with sound. Silence is productive since it causes the candidate to feel pressure to respond. However, response pressure has its limits. If the candidate is not able to respond in about eight to ten seconds, they begin to lose focus on the question and become distracted by the process. At this time, you should step in to relieve the pressure by saying something like "That's okay. Take your time. Think of a good example." This is usually enough to relieve the pressure on the candidate. Even so, pressure will immediately start to build again. If the candidate is still unable to come up with an example, say something like, "That's okay, we'll get back to it" and move on to your next question (don't forget to ask the question again later in the interview).

NOTE : There is a "practice effect" that takes place in a behavior-based interview. Candidates get better at recalling past events as the interview progresses. It's not unusual for a candidate to give you an example later in the interview to a question you asked earlier, but were unable to get a response to.

Interrupt to Maintain Control

Your past socialization training most likely taught you it's not polite to interrupt others while they are speaking. To conduct a quality interview, you *must* interrupt the candidate to maintain control or to get the data you need to make a good hiring decision. If you need more information, if you are unclear about something a job candidate says, or if the candidate is talking too much, don't hesitate to tactfully interrupt. As soon as you start to talk, the candidate will stop to listen.

Seek a Balance

When evaluating a competency, it's always helpful to list the "pros" and "cons" in order to determine which choice will give you the highest payoff. If you draw a vertical line down the center of a piece of paper and list the "pros" in one column and the "cons" in another, you soon will see if the evidence is complete and to what extent the skill is present. However, in order to fairly evaluate the skill, you need evidence in both columns. If the "pro" side is full and the "con" side is empty, the data would be suspect. It's important to get evidence on both sides during the interview. If you are feeling very positive about the candidate you need to seek some balancing negatives. If your feelings are mostly negative, then you need to seek some positive evidence to determine if a skill is present.

It's not difficult to do. Sometimes changing a single word or adding a short phrase to a question will do the trick.

Example:

Original question: "Tell me about a time when you were proud of your ability to stick to company policy."

Revised question: "Tell me about a time you found it necessary to break company policy."

Respect Confidentiality

Many candidates have been exposed to proprietary information in a former job. Expect them to honor their agreement not to disclose confidential information. You can say something like this at the beginning of the interview: "Susan, I would appreciate it if you would answer my questions giving me as much detail as possible. I realize you may have information that is considered confidential. I don't want you to violate any agreements you have made with respect to confidentiality. Just give me as much information as you can within the limits of your agreement."

Here's an example of the application of a few of these techniques from your interview with Susan:

You — "Susan, give me an example of a time when you were able to persuade another person or group to take action on something that was important to you."

Susan — (Looks away, frowns, doesn't say anything)

You — (After about seven seconds have passed with no response) "Susan, I know this is tough. Just take your time. I'm looking for an example of a situation where you were able to persuade someone or a group to take action on something that was important to you."

Susan — (Looks away, after about three seconds, she says) "I've got it! When I first started working at Vertex, I guess it was only after a month, I was asked by my boss to call a meeting of the software department heads in our division. Denise, my boss, wanted to get some agreement on how we might format our software manuals so they would have a consistent look both internally and externally."

You — "So, what did you do?"

Susan — "The first thing I did was to send an email to all software managers letting them know about our desire to hold a meeting. After that, I decided to meet with them personally."

You — "You said you emailed the software managers? Why did you then decide to meet with each one?"

Susan — "I guess my email idea wasn't so great."

You — "Tell me more."

Susan — "Oh, ah — some of them felt I was overstepping my bounds. I didn't set a meeting date or anything like that. All I did was to tell them Denise wanted to get us all together, face-to-face."

You — "What was wrong with that?"

Susan — "I discovered that meetings are the last resort around there. People are so busy they rarely have time."

You — "Help me understand. You said meetings are the last resort, right?" (Susan nods in agreement) "Well then, why would you try to meet with each person individually?"

Susan — "For two reasons. Number one, I hadn't met any of these people. They didn't know me from Adam. I'm much better talking to people face-to-face than through email anyway. The second reason was, I had a strategy in mind. I would pick their brains, and put together some recommendations based on what I learned. After all, I knew..."

You — "Okay, what did you do next?"

Susan — "I started by going to each department and talking to the admin. After that, it was much easier to get on the bosses' calendar."

You — "Easier?"

Susan — "Yes, I found out the admins control the calendars around there."

You — "What happened next?"

Susan — " I met with each department manager."

You — "How many managers are we talking about?"

Susan — "Four."

You — "Go on."

Susan — "I explained what we wanted to do and asked for their recommendations.** Then I wrote up a proposal and gave it to Denise. I told her I had met with the department managers and this was the result. We made a few changes and she sent the proposal out to each department manager."

> **NOTE: At this point you could have chosen to probe more deeply into Susan's method of persuading others to take action. An appropriate question would be: "Susan, focus on just one of those meetings. De-

scribe the details of the conversation you had with one particular department manager."

You — "What happened?"

Susan — "Would you believe, they agreed to meet? Of course they emailed their consent!"

You — "So, how did it turn out?"

Susan — "We had the meeting but couldn't come up with a uniform system. Denise tried to convince everyone to make the changes, but I guess the others let their pride get in the way. I mean, they seemed very territorial. She just dropped the idea after that."

You — "What did you learn from that experience?"

Susan — "The big lesson for me was, do your homework. Looking back on the situation, I should have carried the ball for Denise. I mean, I had a pretty good rapport built up with those managers and I should have held at least one more meeting with each one before we brought them all together. I know my job was to get people to a meeting and I did it. I just felt bad for Denise."

BEHIND THE SCENE

This is what you did that was effective:

☐ Followed your data gathering model (SAFE) and led Susan through it;

☐ Used silence to build productive tension;

☐ Relieved tension when it became unproductive;

☐ Asked for clarification and details many times;

☐ Interrupted Susan to get her back on track;

☐ Paid close attention to Susan's responses and controlled the flow of the interview through comments, questions, and tactful interruption;

☐ Stayed with Susan's example until it reached a logical conclusion.

NOTE: This a situation where the candidate demonstrated the presence of the skill. It might be tempting to evaluate Susan based on the outcome of the meeting. That's not what she was responsible for. Susan brought together five department managers who rarely agree to appear in the same room together. This took some persuasive ability.

You will ask Susan many more questions during this interview.

When you have finished going through your list of prepared questions, take some time to give her information about your company and answer any questions she has. This is the subject of Chapter 11.

Chapter 11

Conduct — Part II

Give the Candidate Information

Review the Organization Structure and the Products or Services

Give the candidate an overview of the company without violating confidentiality requirements. Describe the products or services provided and the role your department plays in creating or supporting them. Explain the working arrangements between your department and the rest of the company. Discuss significant reporting relationships. Identify key groups your new hire will most often be working with.

Describe the Job

If you haven't already done so, review the Essential Job Functions with the candidate. What tasks will a new hire be expected to perform as soon as they come aboard? When will other duties and responsibilities be added? Describe orientation or special training they will receive to help get them up to speed. How much travel is required or are there any special physical requirements or unusual environmental conditions the candidate should know about?

Speaking of unusual environmental conditions: I received an assignment one time to conduct interviewing skills workshops for an oil company in Alaska. Had I known ahead of time about the environmental conditions, I would have either respectfully declined the assignment or at least, raised my fee accordingly! The training took place near the end of October. When I arrived in Anchorage, the temperature was about 38 degrees and I was told this was slightly above normal. The next day, the company put me on an airplane and flew to Dead Horse (an appropriate name) above the Arctic circle. The temperature was a bone-chilling -18 degrees. I stepped off the plane and was hit by a blast of cold air that I was certain could cause severe frostbite in a matter of minutes. I quickly boarded the waiting shuttle bus and we made our way across the frozen tundra to Prudhoe Bay. When the bus driver stopped to let me off at base operations, I wasn't sure I wanted to face that cold air again. The driver confidently told me I could walk the 150 feet to the building entrance. It looked like a scene from a science fiction movie. Here was this building sitting on stilts with nothing but frozen ground all around it. It was far too cold to snow. An ice fog hung in the air and it seemed like the sun could barely creep across the horizon. Well, I built up my courage, grabbed my luggage and stepped from the bus. This time, I was sure I was going to die, but as fate would have it, I made it to the door. I opened the door and entered the building. A security desk was perched at the top of the stairs on the first floor landing. As I checked in, I noticed the outdoor temperature was displayed on the wall behind the desk. It read -55 degrees including the wind chill factor. I spent the next three days being shuttled between a cluster of six buildings, each time having to walk from the building to the bus and back again. I was very thankful it wasn't January.

Characterize the Management and Environment

What kind of supervision will the candidate receive? How much experience has the manager had? What are the manager's strengths? What leadership style does the manager use most often? Describe some of the elements of the work environment (Use these questions as idea stimulators):

☐ Teamwork — is teamwork or individual effort more important in this job?

☐ Pace — is it fast and erratic or slow and steady?

☐ Change — is it rapid and unpredictable or controlled?

☐ Autonomy — is there plenty of freedom to make decisions or are employees required to follow established procedures?

☐ Interaction — will the candidate work alone or with a small or large number of people?

☐ Control — is the candidate told what to do or do they have the freedom to take charge of a situation?

☐ Structure — is the company more conservative or more entrepreneurial, more proactive or reactive?

Cover Salary Range and an Overview of Benefits

If you have a Human Resources professional working with you, they will most likely be the one to deal with this issue. This is an important area to most candidates. It's surprising how many of them will make a career decision based exclusively on these two items. They may not be the best decision criteria in the long run, but candidates are highly influenced by them. So, familiarize yourself with the benefits available. If you can give the candidate a written *summary* of benefits, it will save you some time. They can take the information with them and study it later. The time to describe the benefits in detail is when you present the job offer.

It's rarely necessary to discuss specific compensation arrangements during an interview. Many of these decisions are made just before an offer is presented to the candidate. It's fair to give the candidate an indication of the salary range established for this position. If the range is flexible, give this information to the candidate if you feel it's appropriate. Salary is not the only form of compensation. If you offer stock options, bonuses, etc., you might want to mention these. Indicate that such additional forms of compensation are *possible, not promised*.

Answer Questions

What do candidates want to know about your organization? Sure, the standard stuff like: How are you organized? What are the work hours? What are the benefits? Who will I be working with? What's the salary range? Who's the competition? This is information you, more than likely, have already covered. There are some other questions that your best candidate's may ask. Following are some examples. How would you answer these?

- To what extent do customers hold the company in high esteem?

- What does this company do to support the community?

- Do your products and services promote a clean, healthy environment?

- How does your company demonstrate excellence and quality in all you do?

- Does this company confront intolerance and prejudice whenever it appears?

- Is this company on a firm financial footing?

- What's the near and long-term growth potential for your company and the industry?

- How stable is top management?

- Do people here act with honesty and integrity?

- Do people here trust one another?

- Is teamwork and collaboration valued?

- Do individuals feel valued and respected?

- Who makes the decisions around here?

- Are people treated fairly?

- Is there a "can do" attitude here?

- Will the job be interesting and challenging?

- Will I get the resources I need to do the job?

- Is there opportunity for advancement?

- Will I feel proud to let people know I work here?

- How will my compensation and benefits package be an accurate reflection of my worth?

Sell Your Organization

Tell the candidate why you like working in this organization and what this company means to you. Let them know about your goals, what you value, and what you expect of them.

Ask some open-ended questions like these:

☐ What did you like about your current (or last) job?

☐ What could have made the job even better?

☐ Describe the kind of environment in which you like to work.

Use the candidate's answers to point out the match between their likes and desires with the job they are interviewing for.

Be careful not to oversell or make statements that are untrue.

Let's go back to your interview with Susan:

You — "Well Susan, I know I've asked you a lot of tough questions and I really appreciate your candid responses. But, let me take just a minute to tell you a few things about our company. I've been with Westlake for nearly six years and it's a great company to work for. I've never been in an organization where everyone is willing to do more than their share, all the time. I think that's why we've been profitable and have been able to make it through the lean years. I'm not saying we're perfect, but I wouldn't trade my job for any other. Susan, let me ask you a question. What do you like most about your job?"

Susan — "I'll have to say the freedom. I've been able to experiment — try new things without being worried my boss or anyone else is going to come down on me for it. I also like our team spirit. People seem to be willing to help. Of course, there are a few big egos around. I hope some day they get the message."

You — "I can understand that. One of the joys of working here is the lack of politics. What I mean is, everyone is real honest and straightforward. You never have to be afraid to ask for help — and we all have the freedom to run with the ball. People don't sit around waiting for something to happen. They make things happen!"

Susan — "This sounds like my kind of place. But now, I have a question. How important are titles around here?"

You — "Thanks for asking. The truth is, titles don't mean much at all. I guess they're just a convenient way of trying to show the world we're organized. It's what you do around here that counts, not a title on your business card. You know, 'a rising tide lifts all boats.' We all work together to build a strong and leading edge company."

Susan — "This seems almost too good to be true."

You — "But, it is. Susan let me ask you this: If you could change your job or your company any way you like, what would be different?"

Susan — "I like what you said about titles not getting in the way. I've seen some of that and I think it can make things pretty difficult sometimes. I know my job and I really feel uncomfortable when an executive leans over my shoulder and tells me what to do."

You — "You don't have to worry about that around here. More often than not, they come to us for help and not to give us advice. I really like the fact that this company is driven from the bottom-up, not top-down. Of course you have to understand our customers always come first. Susan, is there anything else you would change?"

Susan — "Yes, I would like a little more time off. Sometimes it feels like I have a twenty-four hour job. I mean, it's not unusual for me to work nine or ten hours a day and then come in on a Saturday or Sunday to finish up an assignment."

You — "That's understandable. I have to tell you, we put in some pretty long hours here ourselves. But, it's worth it. We've received some pretty substantial profit sharing bonuses for our efforts and every so often, we'll declare a 'mental health' day and take an afternoon off for a picnic or barbeque."

BEHIND THE SCENE

This is what you did that was effective:

☐ Gave personal testimony about your admiration for the company;

☐ Admitted the company wasn't perfect, but it's the best you've seen;

☐ Uncovered what Susan liked about her present company and job;

☐ Converted her concerns about politics and titles into a major benefit;

☐ Invited Susan to talk about her dissatisfactions;

☐ Reinforced the notion of equality and participative decision making;

☐ Admitted that long hours would be part of the job, but added the benefits of this requirement.

Close the Interview on a Positive Note

☐ Thank the candidate for her time and for giving you information about her skills.

☐ Give her the "take away" materials you have prepared along with your business card.

☐ Tell her candidate when you will get back to her, and what she should do if you miss your deadline.

☐ Remind the candidate to contact you if she has any questions and especially if she receive an offer before you're back in touch.

☐ Be careful to avoid giving this candidate an indication of how well the interview went and don't make any comments that could be interpreted to mean "you've got the job."

☐ Escort her to the next interview or to the front lobby. It's a nice touch that prevents them from taking a wrong turn, feeling lost, or abandoned.

Your Close:

You — "Well Susan, I guess that about wraps it up. I really enjoyed talking with you today and I hope we'll have an opportunity to work together."

Susan — "It's certainly been a pleasure for me and I'm looking forward to meeting some of the other people here."

You — "Great! Thank you for taking the time to interview with us. I know it's not always easy to get away during the middle of the week. I want you to know I appreciate your willingness to answer my questions and thank you for letting me impose my 'SAFE' model on you."

Susan—"Thank you! I actually found it very helpful. I've never experienced an interview where I had to recall so many experiences. It wasn't easy, but I must admit, it was one of the best interviews I've ever had."

You — "A lot of people find these interviews a little intimidating at first. You gave me exactly the kind of details I needed. Susan, that reminds me, I have some materials for you to take away. Here's a copy of our annual report, a few press clippings, some product literature, and my business card. I hope these are helpful to you. Did I give you a summary of our benefits?"

Susan — "Yes, I have it here."

You—"Okay. As you probably know, we'll be interviewing several candidates for the job of Technical Writer. My guess is we'll finish these no later than Friday of next week. After the interviews are over, we interviewers get together to go over all the information we have and make a hiring decision. So, it looks like we're about two weeks away from a decision. I'll be sure either Wayne or our recruiter lets you know as soon as possible what our decision is. If you don't here from us within two weeks from today, please call either me, Wayne, or Alicia."

Susan — "Okay."

You — "One other thing. If you get an offer from another company before we get back to you, or if you have any questions, please feel free to call me, Alicia, or anyone you've met here."

Susan — "I appreciate that, but I have a question right now. After talking with you, I feel I'm really well qualified for the job. What do you think?"

You — "Susan, the truth is, I don't really know how well qualified you are at this point. I'll evaluate your skills when I go over my notes. Then, I have to talk to the other interviewers. Their input will be as important as mine. I can tell you this. As soon as we've had a chance to interview the other candidates and determine who is the best match for the job, we'll get back to you one way or the other. Now, let's take a walk down the hall to our break room. I'd like to give you a sample of our Westlake hospitality before I introduce you to Mary!"

BEHIND THE SCENE

This is what you did that was effective:

☐ Let her know how much you personally enjoyed talking with her;

☐ Acknowledged the effort she made to come to the interview;

☐ Thanked her for her time;

☐ Acknowledged her ability to handle tough behavior-based interview questions;

☐ Gave her some materials to take away that say positive things about your company;

☐ Let her know what happens after the interviews are over;

☐ Assured her that she would know the outcome within a specific time frame;

☐ Invited her to call with questions or if she receives an offer;

☐ Resisted the temptation to evaluate Susan's skills until you have time to review your notes;

☐ Escorted Susan to the break room and then to her next interview;

☐ Conducted the entire interview process in a professional manner.

With the interview complete, you are ready to review your notes and evaluate the candidate.

In Chapter 12, I'll discuss evaluating the candidate's skills, exchanging data with other interviewers, and making a final decision.

Chapter 12

Evaluate, Exchange and Decide

Evaluate the Job Candidate's Skills

After the candidate has departed, take 20 to 30 minutes to evaluate responses to your structured interview questions. It's best not to proceed to the next interview before you evaluate the information you received in this one. If you conduct two or more interviews in a row and then complete the evaluations, it's highly probable that the information will get mixed and some unintentional cross-over will occur.

Assess skill levels by rating the candidate's answers to your questions. Rate candidates based on the extent to which their skills match the requirements of the job.

Unless these are bona fide requirements for the job and are supported by your job skills analysis, avoid the temptation to rate candidates based on:

☐ First impressions;

☐ Polish;

☐ Intuition;

☐ Personality or friendliness; or

☐ Physical Appearance.

I also recommend that you don't rank-order candidates. Two common errors often take place when interviewers rank-order candidates and make their final hiring decision on that basis:

● Candidates are compared to one another rather than being independently evaluated against the competencies required for the job.

● Ranking gives the appearance that candidates' skill levels are spaced evenly from top to bottom. This illusion could cause you to inadvertently eliminate a qualified candidate (i.e. number three on a list of four) or worse, extend an offer to a less than satisfactory candidate (if your top-ranked candidates are no longer available).

In our behavior-based system, we recommend the *Content Mapping* method because it takes full advantage of all information supplied by the job candidate and it is done immediately following the interview. *Content Mapping* gives you the opportunity to apply data from any of the candidate's answers to any question in order to evaluate a selected competency. It requires, however, that you read all your notes in order to extract the relevant information that applies to the skill you are evaluating. This may sound like a tedious and difficult process, but it really isn't.

Before I explain further, here's a story that illustrates an important point:

> The supervisor of a state department of highway safety hired a young man as a traffic painter.

> On his first day, his supervisor came up to him and said, "Come with me young man, I've got a job for you." They left in the supervisor's pickup truck and went to a lonely stretch of road some 20 miles out of town. The supervisor handed the youngster a six inch wide paint brush, a bucket of paint, and a baseball cap. He said, "What I want you to do is to paint a white line right down the center of this highway, starting here and heading south. I'll be back at the end of the day." The supervisor got in his truck and left.

> He returned at five o'clock. The new employee had painted three miles of white line. "I'm very pleased," he said. "You painted more than I expected and it's straight as an arrow. I'd like you to come back tomorrow."

At the end of the second day, the supervisor once again returned at five o'clock. This time the young man had only painted two miles of white line. The supervisor said, "It's okay. Our average worker paints about two miles of white line a day. I guess you can come back tomorrow."

At the end of the third day, the supervisor returned at five o'clock. This time the young man had only painted one mile of white line. "I'm sorry to tell you this," he said, "but, I'm going to let you go. Tell me son, what happened?" The young man explained. "Sir, the first day was easy, the second day was okay, but today I just got too tired walking all the way back to that darn paint bucket!"

So, why did he fail? He had the technical skill. He just didn't have enough common sense to carry the paint bucket with him!

This story illustrates the *importance of independently evaluating two* distinct *categories of job competencies, Technical Skills and Work Habits.* Your job is to separate information into these two piles. A job holder may demonstrate proficiency in one, both, or neither area. In this case, the young man failed as a result of his ineffective Work Habits.

Often you will get information about *multiple* Work Habits and Technical Skills in the *same* example. Information might be positive, negative, or mixed (as it was in our "traffic line painter" story). Your task is to determine which information is relevant to each competency you are evaluating.

NOTE: A candidate's response to a behavior-based question will contain information about Technical Skills and Work Habits. If you ask a technical question, you will get more Technical Skill data than Work Habit data. And, of course, if you ask a Work Habit question you can expect more Work Habit information.

How to Rate Technical Skills and Work Habits using Content Mapping.

Although there are many techniques for assigning ratings to a job candidate's skills, *Content Mapping* is the most effective and least complicated method for working managers and supervisors. *Content Mapping* is based on the principle of "distributed data", that is, data reflecting the presence or absence of a Work Habit or Technical Skill will be *distributed throughout the entire set of responses to your questions.* This means it will be necessary for you to consult *all* data you have at your disposal when you evaluate competencies a candidate has that are specified in your job requirements.

Follow these steps to rate a candidate's skills:

Refer to the sample Candidate Evaluation Form located in Appendix A (Suggestion: prepare a rating form using the sample on page 233 as a model).

Step 1: Select a single Technical Skill or Work Habit to evaluate.

Step 2: Read the skill definition.

Step 3: Review all notes you have taken during the interview and compare them to the skill definition in order to determine the candidate's skill level.

Step 4: Using the anchors shown on the Job Candidate Evaluation form, circle the appropriate rating.

Step 5: Note the evidence you have to support your evaluation of the competency.

Step 6: Repeat the process for each Technical Skill or Work Habit.

NOTE: Avoid the "horns" or "halo" rating error. That is, if your first few competencies are rated low, you might have a tendency to rate all the others low. Conversely, a high rating on the first one or two, might influence you to erroneously rate all others high.

Rating Skill Practice

This is a short exercise to check your rating ability. Following is an example of one candidate's response to an interview question. Read the information and evaluate the candidate's answer. Record your rating by checking one of the boxes which follow the candidate's response.

Background. This candidate is applying for a position as a Production Section Manager in an equipment manufacturing firm. One of the Work Habits required for this job is *Empowerment.*

Here's the definition:

> **Empowerment**: Ability to build a workplace culture in which people take personal responsibility for making themselves and their organizations successful.

Work Habit Element: Turns people from complainers into problem solvers.

Your question — "Tell me about something you have done in the past to help someone move from a complainer to a problem solver."

Candidate's response — "I was a production manager in a computer company. Our job was to build the cabinets and power supplies. Ray was one of the leads who ran the day shift on the assembly line. I noticed that Ray would often get sick when we were behind schedule or it was the end of the month. At first I thought it was just the pressure. I decided to have a talk with Ray about this. Every time we got behind schedule Ray would start running around like a chicken with its head cut off. Every hour, Ray would come in with a new problem, 'We can't do this, or we can't do that.' he'd say. 'We're short of parts. What's wrong with those guys in production control?' After a day or two of this, Ray would call in sick.

After this had been going on for about three months, I called Ray into my office. I said 'Ray, I can't help noticing that every time we fall behind schedule, you come to see me and tell me you can't do this or that. Ray, in my book, can't means won't. There's always some action you can take to either prevent problems or have a contingency plan in place to get your operation up and running again.' Then I said, 'Ray, how can I help?'

Ray looked at me and said, 'I hate to tell you this, but I don't know how to do that.' I was really surprised! Sure, I had only been in the job a few months myself, but Ray had been there for about three years. So, here's what I did. I had taken a problem solving workshop as part of my management training and I thought this would be an opportunity to see if that stuff really worked. I scheduled some time with Ray and we sat down for about an hour a day for a week just going over the steps of the process. Within a month and a half Ray not only had his production on target, but he stopped coming in to my office to complain about the warehouse people, production control, and anyone else. His attendance got better too. When I asked him about it, he said 'You know, those problem solving techniques really work. I found out something else. Remember how often I was getting sick? Well, guess what? When I got behind I was doing things like going out in the rain without a jacket to chase down parts or crazy things like that. I'd get all worked up and get tied up in knots. With things a lot more under control, I don't feel as much pressure.'"

Your Task

Rate this production manager's ability to help Ray move from a complainer to a problem solver.

Data indicates this candidate's level of competence is:

☐ Substantially less than the job requires

☐ Somewhat less than the job requires

☐ Equal to the job requirement

☐ Somewhat greater than the job requires

☐ Substantially greater than the job requires

Analysis

If you checked "Equal to the job requirement" you are correct. This manager was able to turn Ray's behavior around. Instead of remaining a complainer, Ray became a productive member of this work team. I would bet that not only did productivity improve, but the morale in Ray's work group rose. However, there are acceptable reasons why you might have chosen to rate this candidate differently:

☐ You rated the candidate on only a single behavior-based example. One example is
rarely enough to accurately indicate the skill

level for a given Work Habit or Technical Skill;

☐ You had no opportunity to probe for additional information;

☐ You were not able to see the candidate's body language or listen to the tone of his or her voice;

☐ You didn't know if the change was lasting;

☐ You might have been tempted to rate this candidate lower because three months elapsed before action was taken. However, the desired result was achieved.

Final Thoughts About Evaluation

☐ Rate one competency at a time.

☐ Separate the data to avoid contaminating your rating for a selected competency.

☐ Use more than one interviewer to gather more complete data.

☐ Treat your ratings as tentative until you've talked to the other interviewers.

Exchange and Decide

The final two steps of our "7 Step" PROCEED process should be completed during a meeting attended by all interviewers. Be prepared to modify your hiring decision based on the information exchanged during this meeting.

When all the employment interviews have been completed, arrange a meeting attended by all members of your interview team. This gives you an opportunity to exchange information and may change your opinion about a candidate. Some of my technology clients like to use email for this. The only problem with email is the amount of time required to send messages back and forth. One client is using their "Intranet" to hold meetings and exchange information (an Intranet is an internal communication system where individual computers are connected to each other through a network. With the Intranet, interviewers can participate in interactive conferences. They can send and receive data in real time, but they're sitting in front of a computer monitor).

Complete Evaluation Forms and Review the Ratings for Each Candidate One-By-One.

Start With Any Candidate.

☐ Ask interview team members to share their data and preliminary evaluations with one another and reach consensus on the final evaluation of the candidate for each Technical Skill or Work Habit. Remember, the goal is to use all data you have at your disposal to make an informed decision. If you need more information from a candidate, contact the person by telephone and get what you need or ask them to come in for an additional interview.

Do you remember your interview with Ray's manager? What if another interviewer had asked this question: "Was the change in Ray's behavior permanent or temporary?" The candidate's answer: "I'm sorry to say it only lasted about four months then Ray went right back to his old habits, always whining and complaining. His attendance started to slip, too. It really made me angry and I finally demoted him. I just got sick and tired of it all. They say 'A Leopard can't change his spots.' In Ray's case, I think it's really true. You know, we never got along very well after that."

I'll bet this new information would cause you to re-evaluate this candidate's ability to change people from complainers into problem solvers.

☐ Record final evaluations on a new Job Candidate Evaluation form.

☐ With the completed evaluation form in front of you, estimate the fit between the job requirements and the skills of the candidate and make a decision to either recommend or not recommend this candidate for hire. Some interviewers reduce their ratings to numbers in order to identify the candidate who is best qualified for the job. This practice can be misleading. Remember, if you convert your ratings to numbers, all you accomplish is to quantify judgment. Numbers seem to add precision that, in reality, does not exist. It's best to use "ocular analysis" (just look the data over) along with common sense.

☐ Record the recommendation and your justification on the rating form.

☐ Repeat the process for all remaining candidates.

☐ Finally, compare rating forms and using the combined judgment of your team, select a primary candidate and one or more backup candidates.

Should I Pick the Candidate Who is Overqualified?

Selecting an "overqualified" candidate is a two-edged sword. It's more cost effective to select for competencies than it is to develop them. So, reason tells us to select the candidate who is promotable (i.e. overqualified). Unfortunately there is evidence to show that overqualified people fail in jobs as often as under qualified people. It seems that overqualified people often focus attention on incorrect parts of the job.

For example: a manager who is highly skilled in Team Building and Collaboration may fail to act decisively and take charge in a crisis situation. There is also a danger that the overqualified candidate will become frustrated or bored unless this person receives assignments that challenge their ability and require that they perform at the highest levels.

A logical counter-argument at this point is: "I plan to promote this person to a higher level job in one or two years."

If this is your argument, the candidate is (in reality) NOT overqualified provided you have clearly identified this position as "interim" BEFORE you began interviewing candidates.

Many seniors who are nearing retirement or are returning to the workforce are a noted exception to the failure rate of overqualified employees. These workers are less motivated by security, advancement, and status than most younger workers. Their maturity and wealth of experience are valuable assets.

The final decision is yours, but I recommend you select candidates whose skill levels most closely match the requirements of the job, being neither significantly under qualified or overqualified.

> Note: Sometimes your primary candidate has accepted another position or does not choose to accept your offer. For that rea-son, you should be prepared to offer the po-sition to a qualified backup candidate

Chapter 13 covers post-interview activities.

Chapter 13

Final Steps

Complete Background and Reference Checks

Reference checking has become more difficult over the years due to concern by companies over potential lawsuits caused by employees who give false or damaging information about former employees to inquiring parties. Many companies have policies prohibiting the release of information other than dates of employment and job title. Often a call to a supervisor results in a referral to the human resources department.

Suggestions. Here are some suggestions on how to overcome these obstacles:

☐ Obtain *written* permission from the candidate to conduct reference checks;

☐ Ask the candidate to help you in obtaining information from references by:

   1. Impressing upon them the need for reference checking. Without favorable references, there can be no job offer.

   2. Ask the candidate to telephone each reference to let the reference know what they can say about them (It makes the candidate feel comfortable, but references will tell you what they want you to hear anyway).

When you telephone the candidate's references:

☐ Identify yourself, your company, and the position the candidate is applying for;

☐ Confirm that the reference has been contacted by the candidate and has given the reference provider permission to speak with you;

☐ Promise confidentiality and keep your promise;

☐ Take notes;

☐ Determine the nature of the relationship between the candidate and the reference provider;

☐ Ask open-ended questions about events the candidate has described to you in the interview;

☐ Follow-up open-ended questions with probes to uncover details or to clarify information;

☐ Ask references to provide you with names of other people you may talk to about this candidate.

Background checks. Not checking a candidate's background can be dangerous and legally risky. Juries are rewarding petitioners (customers, co-workers, and the general public) with big settlements for injuries or damage caused by hires who would not have been chosen if the employer had taken the time to do a thorough background check and learn about a person's history. Judges are unwilling to accept "I tried" as an excuse for failure to uncover a person's past dangerous behaviors.

In addition to contacting former employers, verify educational information by calling the institutions listed in the candidate's résumé or on the application form. Exaggerating education is common among applicants who stretch the truth.

The Fair Credit Reporting Act (FCRA) permits you to obtain information about an applicant's credit without getting their permission. This should only be done if the job requires a person to handle large sums of money or to control substantial liquid assets. If you discover a candidate has filed for bankruptcy, you cannot use this information for rejecting the person unless you are able to demonstrate the actions which led to the bankruptcy reflect a lack of competency as indicated by the duties and responsibilities of the job.

You can engage the services of an investigator to check driving and criminal records. Most states will provide driving records, but access to criminal records may be restricted on a "need-to-know" basis. Information contained in federal crime files is available only to banks and other selected institutions.

Extend the Offer

It's customary in many organizations for the hiring manager to extend a verbal offer to the selected candidate following completion of reference checks, background checks, and review of benefits such as salary, vacation, stock, bonus, and relocation expectations. Telephone the candidate and get a verbal commitment and a tentative start date. Immediately follow-up the verbal offer with a confirmation letter containing complete details. Specify the amount of time the offer is valid (usually three to five business days) and request the return of a signed copy. Review the content of the letter to make sure it contains no language that can be interpreted as an offer of permanent employment. Do include language that welcomes the candidate to your organization. The offer may be made contingent upon a satisfactory physical exam and proof of authorization to work in the United States. Reference checks, if not completed, may also be included as a contingency.

When you have received the signed copy and are certain the person is coming aboard, notify those candidates who were not chosen. Every candidate who was interviewed should receive a response. It's up to you to decide if you want to personally telephone each one, but all candidates should be sent a personalized letter that informs them of your decision. Above all, design your letters to reflect your organization's reputation as a great place to work.

Bring the New Employee on Board

Getting your new employee off to a good start is important. You only have one chance to make a good first impression. You probably can remember some of the orientation processes you experienced when you first reported for a new job. Would you like your new employee to get the same kind of reception you received? Look at the process from the new employee's point of view. If this were you, what would impress you? How would you like to be treated? What information would you need? Who would you like to meet? What would you want others to do to help you become an accepted member of the team?

New employees need extra help in getting adjusted to a new environment. It takes time for them to understand the "corporate culture" and how things get done.

Charlotte's First Day

I was brought in to prepare a new hire orientation program for a client in the telecommunications industry.

The first thing I did was interview a new hire so I could get a sense of what was needed.

I met with Charlotte after her first day on the job. My first question was: "Charlotte, tell me about your day." She looked at me and said, "Do you really want to know about it?" "Absolutely" I replied. "Okay," she said, "I wish my boss was here to meet me this morning. I didn't even know what building to report to. The receptionist in building three couldn't help me and I had to wander around until I found Ken's office. I finally got there and he was nowhere to be found. I told his secretary I was reporting for work, but she didn't seem to know anything about me. She got up from her desk and went into somebody's office, I think his name was Steve. Anyway, he came out and said, 'Oh, I guess you're the new kid on the block. Ken's off to a budgeting meeting and I don't know exactly when he'll be back. There's an empty office next to mine. Why don't you take that one?' I did. I just sat there for about an hour, doing nothing. I mean, it would have been nice if I at least had a telephone, or a pencil, or maybe a waste basket. Steve finally came into my office with a stack of manuals. He plopped them on my desk and said, 'Here, these should keep you busy for awhile.' So, I spent most of the day reading about procedures, standards, and manufacturing processes."

"Did anyone take you to lunch?" I asked. "Are you kidding?" she said. "I didn't see a soul the rest of the day. I'll tell you what I did. About noon, I just got up, and started roaming the halls until I managed to find a small break room. I bought some fruit from a vending machine and that was lunch. I went back to the office and just kept reading. At four thirty, I asked the secretary if she would escort me here for my meeting with you. She told me she was sorry but she had to pick up her kids right away. She gave me a site map and pointed out the location of this building."

"It sounds like this has been a pretty trying day," I said.

Charlotte replied, "Yes, I wish I had at least seen my boss. But, — I'll be back tomorrow."

Charlotte's experience was not unusual. As part of the new orientation program, I developed a checklist similar to the one shown below. Feel free to use it as a starting point to build your own.

Welcome Aboard Checklist

☐ Make sure your new employee's work area is ready for them before they arrive.

☐ Personally greet your new employee when they first arrive, even if he or she is required to attend an orientation the first morning.

☐ Review the agenda for the orientation period.

☐ Tour the facilities and introduce your new employee to some of the people he or she will be interacting with.

☐ Complete paperwork required to establish a personnel file and comply with legal requirements.

☐ Provide a brief overview of your industry, your organization, your department.

☐ Review the goals and objectives of your department, and your new employee's role. Include duties, responsibilities, authority, and their relationship to others in the department, to clients, and customers. Discuss policies, practices and "house rules."

☐ Introduce your new employee to a "partner" who can help this person adjust to the job and new surroundings.

☐ Together with your new employee, work out a plan that details how this person can become productive as soon as possible. Provide whatever support and resources are needed to insure this person succeeds.

☐ Take your new employee to lunch.

☐ Meet with your new hire at the end of the day to answer questions and prepare a plan for the balance of their orientation period.

Chapter 14

Short and Final

This is the last chapter in the book and the shortest. If you've stayed with me this long, you deserve some consideration.

Even though the material I have included in this book is based on years of research and practical experience, it can always be improved. I encourage you to experiment with the methods and discover what works best for you. I believe you now have an excellent set of tools to get you started. The cardinal rule is to *stay legal* and *play fair*. The *best* thing you can do is put someone in a job where their competencies closely match the requirements. The *worst* thing you can do is the opposite. You will suffer, your organization will suffer, and most of all, the jobholder will suffer. The wrong job can break a person's spirit, sometimes for life. The right job can be the gateway to fulfillment, growth and satisfaction. Do your best to match the person to the job.

Here's a True Story

Bill was a compensation analyst is a semiconductor company. I joined the company in 1981 and Bill worked for a colleague of mine. Bill was a big guy, yet easy to talk to. The only time he got upset was when he had to negotiate a compensation package with a hiring manager, which seemed to be most of the time. Bill defended his position with gusto. He would argue at the drop of a hat. I watched him stand toe-to-toe with directors and vice presidents. He would get his nose an inch or two from his "opponent" and fight as hard as he could to hold his ground. Of course Bill lost more often than he won because he was always out-ranked. People must have respected him, because he was a ten-year veteran of these corporate gunfights.

It took its toll on Bill. You could see it in his eyes and the way he walked, kind of bent over a little. His boss, who had been on board for about three years, finally had it with Bill. I know he wanted to fire him.

About that time, one of the operating divisions needed a human resources manager to replace a person who had transferred to a facility in Texas. Bill was given the job.

A miraculous change came over Bill. Now he was on the other side of the fence. He loved it! The people he worked for loved it! Bill flourished. When I left the company in 1986, Bill was promoted to Corporate Director of Human Resources. He's been doing a magnificent job ever since. He might have been in the right job to start with, but clearly it wasn't right for him anymore.

Someone should have helped him make a move a lot sooner. But what about Bill? Shouldn't he have done something to help himself. Of course, but Bill didn't even realize what had happened to him. It was a slow process that took place over a number of years. It cost the company through lost productivity, and Bill paid the price in stress, poor health, and loss of self esteem. We all have something to learn from Bill's experience. Putting a "warm body" in a job rather than putting forth the effort it takes to find the right person can be a very expensive way to go.

Build Your Skills Through Practice

It takes practice to become proficient in anything you do. As you gain experience with the "7 Step" PROCEED process, you will be able to combine "skill" with "technology." The interview process requires a lot of skill. You must be a good listener, adaptable, assertive, a collaborator, think critically, make good decisions, be decisive, dedicated, empathic, demonstrate integrity, manage diversity, plan, organize, schedule, be sociable, speak effectively, build an effective team, and be versatile. This requires the effective use of about 21 Work Habits! The technology is here in this book. If you follow the process I have outlined you will get fantastic results — even if you haven't yet mastered the necessary Work Habits.

My First Behavior-Based Interview

When I conducted my first behavior-based interview it went something like this:

(Reconstructed from entries in my journal of 5-21-82)

Failure was something I dreaded most as I interviewed Dale for the job of Staff Trainer. It was the very first time I tried to use a behavior-based system to interview a job candidate. How am I doing, I wondered? Is it going okay? Am I sticking to my plan? I watched Dale's facial and body reactions to the questions I was asking and strained to listen to what he was saying. I struggled to take notes and to appear unemotional and cool. All the time I was concerned about the outcome. After about 15 minutes something magical seemed to happen. Dale was telling me things I thought I would never hear. He was describing a situation where he really fouled things up. I couldn't believe what I was hearing. What a revelation. I knew right then and there, this technique really works. I was ecstatic. I hoped Dale could not see beneath my façade. I didn't want him to know that I was overjoyed at having discovered this incredible new power.

Was my interview technique perfect? Not by a long shot. And yes, I was concerned about how it would go the very first time. After all, I didn't want to look like I didn't know what I was doing. Soon after the interview began I discovered that my prepared questions were all I needed to carry me through.

It was awesome. I really enjoyed that first interview. I decided at that moment, I had to learn all I could about behavior-based interviewing.

That was in 1982. I've learned a lot since then and all I have learned, I offer to you. The system works. It takes just a few interviews to really get the hang of it. Stick with it and it will serve you well. There's an old adage attributed to the Indians of the southwest. It goes something like this: *The greatest gift, is the gift of learning, and it is not complete until it is passed on.* It seems to me, you now have a job do. That is, help the people who work alongside you learn this methodology. Then they, like you, will have the power to make the best hiring decision every time.

You might be wondering if Dale got the job. He didn't, but he let me know my interview was the most professional he had ever experienced. That made me feel very good.

Good luck and good hiring.

Call me with your questions or comments. I can be reached at (949) 661-1669. My email address is: Del@HireUP.com.

Appendix A

Sample Forms

Job Description Planner

Evaluation Form

Sample Job Description Planner first page

Job Description Planner   **Page 1**

Prepared by: Del J. Still   **Date:**   **Job Title:**
Programmer, personal computers, data base applications.

Main Purpose: The main purpose for this job is to write complete data base software applications for in house personal computer users. Responsibilities include all phases from receiving user requests, project planning and design, writing code, testing code, final installation, and ongoing program maintenance for all users.

Job Functions (List all and indicate those that are essential):

1. *Converts data from project specifications and statements of problems and procedures to create or modify computer programs.
2. *Prepares or receives from Systems Analyst detailed work flow charts and diagrams to illustrate the sequence of steps that a program must follow and to describe input, output, and logical operations involved.
3. *Analyzes work flow chart and diagrams, applying knowledge of computer capabilities, subject matter and symbolic logic in order to create efficient applications.
4. *Confers with supervisors and representatives of departments concerned with the program to resolve questions of program intent, data input, output requirements, and inclusion of internal checks and controls.
5. *Converts detailed logical flow charts into data base programs which can be processed by the computer.
6. May train users of the program in order to insure they are able to effectively apply it to their situation.
7. May assist the user to resolve problems in running computer programs on their hardware.
8. *May work with Systems Analyst to obtain and analyze project specifications and flow charts.

* = Essential

Example for First Three Essential Job Functions
(Use as many sheets as required to cover all functions)

Job Description Planner   Page 2

Essential Job Function: Converts data from project specifications and statements of problems and procedures to create or modify computer programs.

Technical Skills: Knowledge of capacities and limitations of Visual Basic. Knowledge of Object Oriented, Client/Server, event-driven, data-dictionary enabled applications development.

Work Habits: Compliance, Critical Thinking, Written Communications

---

Essential Job Function: Prepares or receives from Systems Analyst detailed work flow charts and diagrams to illustrate the sequence of steps that a program must follow and to describe input, output, and logical operations involved.

Technical Skills: Able to create logic diagrams and flow charts that utilize the benefits of object oriented programming to create fast and efficient programs. Ability to read and interpret complex flow charts and schematics.

Work Habits: Analysis, Compliance, Written Communications

Essential Job Function: Analyzes work flow chart and diagrams, applying knowledge of computer capabilities, subject matter and symbolic logic in order to create efficient applications.

Technical Skills: Up-to-date knowledge of available PC platforms and Client/Server hardware. Able to determine which data base product(s) will provide the optimal solution for a given client application.

Work Habits: Analysis, Critical Thinking

Last Page of Job Description Planner

Job Description Planner	Page3

Experience, education and training: Three to five years experience in data base programming including in-depth knowledge of Visual Basic. Requires BSCS or equivalent experience. Proven ability to work effectively in an autonomous or team environment and experience in managing moderately complex projects, including customer interface, design, development, installation, customer orientation, troubleshooting and on-going technical support.

Reporting relationships: Reports to Manager, Corporate Information Services

Special requirements:

Other information: Key Work Habits for this position: Acumen, Analysis, Collaboration, Compliance, Critical Thinking, Customer Satisfaction, Dedication, Written Communications.

Sample form with competencies listed
Ratings have not yet been assigned

Job Candidate Evaluation Form

Candidate: _____   Date: _____

Job Title: Programmer, Personal Computers

Interviewed by: _____

Rating Key: Candidate's level of competence
A = Substantially less than the job requires
B = Somewhat less than the job requires
C = Equal to the job requirement
D = Somewhat greater than the job requires
E = Substantially greater than the job requires
U = Unable to evaluate

Technical Skills	**Rating**	
Capacities/limitations xbase languages	A B C D E	U
Knowledge of client/server, etc.	A B C D E	U
Create logic diagrams/flow charts	A B C D E	U
Read/interpret flow charts/schematics	A B C D E	U
Hardware knowledge	A B C D E	U
Specify optimal xbase product(s)	A B C D E	U
Apply CASE, other PC tools	A B C D E	U
Evaluate specifications/flow charts	A B C D E	U

Work Habits	**Rating**	
Acumen	A B C D E	U
Analysis	A B C D E	U
Critical Thinking	A B C D E	U
Collaboration	A B C D E	U
Compliance	A B C D E	U
Customer Satisfaction	A B C D E	U
Dedication	A B C D E	U
Written Communications	A B C D E	U

Recommendation: __ Hire ___Don't Hire ___ Need More Data
Add comments to support your recommendation on reverse side.

Appendix B

Work Habit Definitions

Definitions are arranged in alphabetical order.

Acumen

Ability to deal effectively with organizational politics and build alliances with people at all organizational levels.

Understands the agendas and perspectives of others; effectively balances the needs of self and one's own work group with the key objectives, values and mission of the broader organization; able to judge which goals are worth fighting for and when it's best to compromise or "give in"; is seen as primarily committed to the organization rather than promoting personal gain; knows the right things to say at the right times; knows when to lead and when to follow; anticipates others reactions or positions accurately; has good timing; involves the right people at the right time; "pre-sells" ideas to key people before introducing them to the whole organization; effectively uses formal and informal channels to achieve results.

Adaptability

Ability to demonstrate flexibility in dealing with difficult or unpleasant circumstances, or adjusting to changing conditions, in order to meet job requirements.

Shows resilience in the face of conflict, frustrating circumstances, constraints, rapidly changing circumstances, shifting priorities, adversity, and multiple demands upon time and other resources; has a high tolerance of ambiguity; does not become defensive when receiving feedback from others, but instead uses feedback as a tool to do a better job; works well under stress and pressure; able to identify the critical needs in a situation, deal with those, and put the others on the "back burner."

Analysis

Ability to gather information and extract relevant data and apply it to a current situation in order to arrive at a conclusion, solve a problem, or make a valid decision.

Uses a systematic approach, seeking input from a variety of sources, being aware of the complexities of the situation; effectively applies principles of inductive or deductive logic; consults print-based or computer-based media; gathers information from individuals and groups; sets limits on data gathering time in order to arrive at a timely decision; uses flowcharts, maps, or network diagrams to help others visualize the interrelationships among data elements; conducts "what-if" analyses to test hypotheses; may employ computer modeling techniques; may use a formal problem-solving method to determine root causes of a problem; able to check self and other's logic in order to determine the validity of the conclusion or decision.

Assertiveness

Ability to express oneself in a confident manner and maintain a point of view even while experiencing opposition.

Able to achieve the intended result by being persistent without being abusive, violating the rights of others, or verbally attacking another person; able to maintain self esteem while being criticized by others; keeps a positive mental attitude which supports the achievement of goals and objectives; able to say "no" to unreasonable demands of others; does not hesitate to ask for resources; questions authority in a tactful way; is results-oriented and has high personal drive; willing to ask tough questions to get necessary information; is not threatened by conflict and manages disagreements well.

Coaching

Ability to evaluate the development needs of employees and provide guidance in improving current job performance or preparing for career advancement.

Able to recognize jobholder's areas of strength as well as areas where development is needed; encourages jobholder to be proactive in improving their performance or preparing for advancement; provides challenging and meaningful assignments; creates the proper conditions which foster professional growth; assists employees in building a development plan; suggests resources such as potential mentors and training opportunities; provides employees with information about available positions in the organization that is consistent with the employee's career goals; gives employees opportunities to be exposed to other parts of the organization; monitors day to day work performance and provides regular performance feedback to jobholders; gives employees feedback that is specific and behavioral rather than judgmental; does not punish mistakes, instead, uses them as opportunities for problem-solving.

Collaboration

Ability to work effectively with others in order to achieve meaningful results.

Displays a willingness to establish alliances and partnerships which may involve the modification of individual needs for the good of the group; responds both assertively and cooperatively, actively participating in seeking results which benefit all parties in making plans, solving problems, making decisions, completing tasks, and accomplishing goals; does not use personal or position power to satisfy one's own needs at the expense of others; communicates a willingness to consider the suggestions and ideas of others; clarifies and communicates agreements, action plans, and goals in order to assure understanding.

Commitment to Quality

Ability to champion the need to deliver quality products and services; to maintain the issue of quality as a primary organizational focus, and to support the concept of "Total Quality Management."

Actively builds strategic alliances with suppliers, vendors, and customers; defines quality standards based on customer requirements instead of internally developed specifications; views quality as the responsibility of everyone in the organization; ensures that continuous improvement is in place in all systems and processes; develops specific goals, strategic and tactical plans to achieve quality leadership; trains employees in the techniques of quality; works with both internal and external customers to establish quality standards and procedures to measure success; accepts only excellence from vendors and suppliers; fixes quality problems immediately and develops processes or procedures to prevent reoccurrence; recognizes and rewards quality improvement efforts as well as successes.

Compliance

Ability to follow established guidelines, policies, and procedures in order to ensure consistency or to protect the safety or preserve the welfare of others.

Understands the necessity for complying with regulations, following procedures or enforcing policies; may use checklists, flowcharts, or decision trees to follow a prescribed sequence; thoroughly and accurately fills out required forms and documents; able to stick to an established routine over a long period of time; does not act on impulse; tends to avoid risk; not easily persuaded to make exceptions to policies and guidelines; applies policies, and regulations consistently to those at all levels within the organization; calls upon higher authority when an exception to a regulation or policy is needed.

Conflict Management

Ability to work with people at all levels in the organization to create effective solutions and maintain positive working relationships when disagreements arise.

Brings conflict out into the open, does not avoid it or sacrifice own needs in order to placate others; uses facts, not personalities, to reach a decision when an argument develops within the work group; views disagreements as healthy expressions of differing viewpoints from which better ideas and solutions can be obtained; bases decisions about conflict resolution on the quality of the ideas presented rather than on the position a person holds; questions everyone thoroughly in order to uncover the reasons behind a disagreement, determines what each party wants to accomplish, and integrates the best ideas into an acceptable resolution; uses systematic problem solving techniques to identify the real causes underlying a conflict; uses collaboration whenever possible to build win-win solutions to conflicts; uses mediation or direct confrontation to deal with power struggles and to resolve win-lose situations; prevents recurrences of conflicts.

Critical Thinking

Ability to examine information, facts, and data, and make valid judgments based on content and quality.

Uses logic to support judgments; makes timely and appropriate decisions under conditions of uncertainty; recognizes when assumptions have been made and whether they are logically valid or invalid based on available evidence; able to determine if arguments are strong or weak; able to draw logical conclusions from available information; fully understands the business and its priorities and factors both hard data and respect for people into the analysis and decision-making process; weighs the known against the unknown, predicting benefits and costs, and weighing risks; controls impulsiveness, yet knows when to take immediate action; does not procrastinate unnecessarily.

Customer Satisfaction

Ability to build productive relationships with internal or external customers in order to build customer loyalty and business success.

Identifies or anticipates customer needs, regularly sets standards that exceed customer specifications, keeps commitments to customers, encourages and uses customer feedback to improve service; treats both internal and external customers with the same high level of respect; effectively communicates the commitment to customer satisfaction to other parts of the organization; rewards others who provide exemplary customer service; trains others in customer service techniques; measures customer satisfaction through surveys, reports, or other tools; takes responsibility for mistakes in delivery or quality of product or service and atones for the errors; responds in a timely manner to customer phone calls, complaints, and inquiries.

Decision Making

Ability to systematically evaluate the positives and negatives of competing choices in order to select the most appropriate alternative.

Able to clearly specify what has to be decided and what result is to be achieved by the decision; determines which criteria are absolutely essential for an alternative in order to be included in the final selection process; identifies which criteria are desirable, but not absolutely essential; applies a form of benefit or numerical analysis to evaluate the relative strengths of alternatives; designs or utilizes tools such as tables, charts, or graphs in order to support a rational decision; weighs the "pros" and "cons" of each alternative to determine which choice has the highest payoff; may present findings to others in a formal presentation or through a written report.

Decisiveness

Ability to make a decision based on available information and assume the risks involved in order to achieve a desired result.

Able to respond to the imminent need to make a decision and not cause unnecessary delay; not overly influenced by the need to make the "popular" decision; resists compromise if the desired result will not be achieved; knows when it is necessary to make exceptions to the rules or modify established policies and procedures; responds effectively to crises or emergency situations.

Dedication

Ability to fully invest oneself in the job and exhibit a high level of commitment; often makes personal sacrifices in order to get the job done or to handle a temporary increase in workload.

Able to stick to a task or pursue a goal in the presence of obstacles or other difficulties; sets high personal standards; places job accomplishment high on the priority list; able to tolerate repetitive tasks over long hours; able to maintain enthusiasm in spite of changing priorities, recurring problems, and resource limitations; actively seeks out difficult and challenging assignments; works long hours when necessary; takes the initiative to go beyond what is expected; emphasizes results and focuses on continuous improvement; takes the initiative regarding job functions and responsibilities; demonstrates a high level of commitment to the organization through words and actions.

Empathic Listening

Ability to listen attentively and to fully and deeply understand a person on an emotional as well as on an intellectual level.

Able to go beyond popular skill-based techniques such as "active" or "reflective" listening which focus on the intent to reply, control, or manipulate; listens not only with the ears but also with eyes and heart; listens for feelings, meaning, and behavior; uses sensing and intuition — i.e., both sides of the brain; seeks first and foremost to understand before trying to be understood; displays a willingness to change an action, opinion, belief, principle, or value based on what is understood; avoids giving advice or evaluating the ideas of another person; avoids trying to "figure out" another person or discover "why" they feel the way they do.

Empowerment

Ability to build a workplace culture in which people take personal responsibility for making themselves and their organization successful.

Actively promotes an "entrepreneurial spirit" within the organization; gives others the latitude to manage their own responsibilities and the authority necessary to accomplish their objectives; maintains high expectations for performance; fosters independent thinking and decision making; dispenses discipline and constructive criticism appropriately and impartially; turns people into problem solvers; acts with integrity; sees oneself as a positive force for change and improvement; acts in a positive political manner without being manipulative; effectively challenges the bureaucratic status quo and its pressures to be safe, cautious, and compliant.

Goal Setting

Ability to set goals for oneself or others that are realistic, time bound, describe the desired result, comprehensive, and stated plainly enough to be understood.

Ensures that individual goals are compatible with organizational goals; establishes sub goals within a long-term goal; ensures that goals are realistic and based on available resources and other priorities; weighs the merits of individual vs. group goal setting and uses each type where appropriate; describes exactly what result is expected when the goal is achieved; uses goal-setting as a positive tool for helping oneself and others learn new skills to improve quality and productivity; periodically holds progress review sessions to measure progress and modify goals, or to identify or remove barriers to goal attainment.

Information Management

Ability to evaluate the requirements of the organization for information and to provide information on a timely basis.

Gives the appropriate people in the organization the information they need when they need it; communicates changes and decisions in a timely manner; gathers data from internal sources such as operating departments and staff organizations; gathers data from external sources such as government agencies, trade and professional associations, journals, periodicals, newsletters, computerized data bases and systems; utilizes a computerized or manually based management information system to gather, store, and distribute data needed by the organization for planning, control, and decision making; ensures information provided is useful, timely, and affordable.

Influence

Ability to persuade others to take a course of action or to alter their opinions in the absence of direct authority over them.

Gains support and commitment from others; mobilizes them to take action; able to present a point of view in a forceful way without offending others; presents compelling reasons to support proposals and ideas; displays energy and enthusiasm in the process of achieving goals; creates a positive "self-fulfilling prophecy" about what can be achieved; rewards people in tangible and intangible ways for the efforts they put forth; works collaboratively with others to achieve results; well connected with important people inside or outside the organization; can be relied upon to keep promises and commitments.

Innovation

Ability to generate creative or original solutions to apply to new and existing situations or to tap the creative genius within one's people or customers.

Constantly experiments with new ways to improve on "what is"; determines when innovation is appropriate, as opposed to more traditional approaches; effectively utilizes existing information rather than always "reinventing the wheel"; enjoys playing with ideas and concepts; likes to explore and solve problems; intellectually curious; displays a "can-do" attitude when faced with a temporary impasse; fosters a climate where others feel free to experiment and express ideas without fear of criticism; blends logical and intuitive processes; removes burdensome bureaucracy; challenges those elements of the corporate culture that endorse conformity and compliance and support "the way it has always been done"; permits freedom in allowing others to determine "how to" do things.

Integrity

Ability to maintain firm adherence to values and principles even in the face of significant pressure to compromise.

Keeps promises and commitments; maintains confidences when asked to do so; describes things as they really are, does not cover up, falsify information or stretch the truth; can be trusted; does not take advantage of another person's weaknesses; does not ask more of others than asks of oneself; does not put people in situations where they could be harmed; is fully accountable for words and actions and takes responsibility for mistakes; shares rewards and recognition with those who contribute to one's success; shows respect for and confidence in employees; demonstrates willingness to make tough decisions.

Leadership

Ability to establish a meaningful vision that defines organizational purpose and through exemplary behavior, expertise, and personal power, directs the thinking and actions of others in order to achieve the desired result.

Stimulates people to stretch and grow, while helping them to overcome obstacles; helps others gain confidence and build commitment to the organization's mission; is a model of integrity and hard work — sets high work expectations for self and others; commands the attention and the respect of people at all organizational levels; challenges others to make tough choices and supports them when they do; acts as a catalyst for change and continuous improvement; clarifies roles and responsibilities for members of the team; provides clear direction and sets priorities for the team; helps others grow and develop by providing training opportunities and challenging assignments.

Managing Change

Ability to initiate, implement and promote change in the organization in order to create new business opportunities, meet market demands, develop new technology, respond to customer or employee needs, or maintain continuous improvement efforts.

Involves those who are most effected by the change in the planning and implementation process; clearly communicates the purpose, vision, roles, responsibilities, and implementation schedule to those involved; readily shares information with others and is available to address concerns or answer questions; communicates both the gains and losses which accompany a change; anticipates resistance to change and demonstrates a willingness to deal with it as a problem to be solved rather than a personality flaw; creates transition plans to proactively manage change; works with other advocates of change in the organization to initiate and support change efforts; actively monitors the change process through two-way communication with others; develops ways to reward those who accept change management as a basic part of their job; educates others in the organization about change and how to effectively manage it; demonstrates support, enthusiasm, and commitment to change.

Managing Diversity

Ability to recognize and effectively employ differences among people in a manner that demonstrates respect for the individual while at the same time achieving the required result.

Through words and actions, fosters appreciation for individual differences regardless of a person's interests, values, lifestyle, race, religion, color, disability, gender, or background;. avoids responding with stereotypical behaviors based on habit, conditioning or socialization; looks beyond personal prejudices to appreciate differences; views differences among people as an opportunity for learning new approaches to work; develops and promotes an atmosphere where it is safe for all employees to ask for help; ensures that the physical work environment represents diversity; willingly accommodates the special needs of the disabled; confronts racist, sexist and other comments that attack the self-respect of others; develops consensus on the core values of the organization and builds a balance between shared values and differences; builds on the complementary skills of the diverse team in order to utilize the full potential of all employees; advocates system and policy changes that are sensitive to the needs of a diverse work force.

Motivation

Ability to create a desire in others to perform at a high level or to modify their attitudes through the use of role modeling, positive reinforcement, and incentives.

Encourages employees to set ambitious goals; serves as a positive role model by performing at a high level of excellence; recognizes the achievements of employees in a manner that shows pride in them and demonstrates support; provides opportunities for others to pursue those activities which excite them; looks for opportunities to catch people in the act of doing something right and provides immediate reinforcement; works at building "spirit" within the work unit; clearly communicates performance expectations to each employee; removes barriers within the work system that prevent employees from effectively performing their jobs; expresses trust in employees competence to do their job; redesigns jobs to make them more satisfying; gives employees more authority and accountability; provides employees with the resources needed to do their jobs.

Organizing

Ability to develop an effective organizational structure, recruit and hire a competent staff, and develop systems, processes, and procedures in order to achieve high quality output.

Analyzes one's organization, looking at reporting relationships and distribution of responsibilities and making changes as necessary; analyzes work flow and operations performed to eliminate bottlenecks, duplication, and improve efficiency; standardizes work processes using tools such as flowcharts, project planning worksheets and meeting guidelines; examines reward systems, performance planning and review systems, training programs, and information systems to ensure that they support the vision and mission of the organization; purchases new technology or equipment to reduce the labor content of work; studies other organizations to get ideas on how to improve one's own organization; determines required staffing level, provides justification, recruits and hires staff.

Planning and Scheduling

Ability to develop short and long range plans that are comprehensive, realistic, and effective in achieving established objectives.

Evaluates the current situation before attempting to develop a plan; links operational plans to the organization's strategic goals and direction; is sensitive to resource and time constraints; determines type and amount of resources necessary to implement a plan; integrates planning efforts across organizational units; gives proper attention to both day-to-day activities and longer range plans; involves others in the planning process; determines how overall progress will be measured; may incorporate formal project management tools such as "Work Breakdown Tables", "Project Master Schedules", "Network Diagrams", and "Responsibility Charts"; able to troubleshoot plans by identifying potential problems, assessing threat, developing either preventive or contingent actions; prioritizes work.

Problem Solving

Ability to systematically organize and evaluate information in order to determine the true cause of a problem and apply corrective action.

Avoids "jumping to solution" until the problem has been clearly defined, relevant facts and data have been gathered, potential causes have been developed, and a most likely cause has been identified; takes interim actions as necessary to deal with the immediate effects of a problem; does not take action based solely on "gut feelings" or "best guesses"; looks for the simpler, more practical causes of a problem before testing the more esoteric causes; uses some type of verification strategy to establish a problem's true cause.

Sociability

Ability to approach and interact with others in a warm, friendly, and supportive manner, creating a climate of trust, consideration, and mutual respect.

Responsive to the needs of others for acceptance, warmth, sensitivity or harmony; able to establish rapport even under difficult circumstances; a good mixer; enjoys the company of others; able to accurately read another's nonverbal behaviors in order to understand one's feelings; easy to approach and talk to; frequently contacted by others for advice or support; proactive in speaking to and maintaining contacts with others; develops an extensive network of contacts; regularly attends social events in order to meet and converse with new people; establishes trust by maintaining confidentiality when asked to do so; diplomatic in interacting with others; places high value on face-to-face communication.

Spoken Communications

Ability to effectively present ideas, transmit information, or convey concepts to individuals or groups of people of varying educational, cultural, and experience levels.

Able to modify the way one communicates in order to minimize the possibility that the message will be misinterpreted; avoids overuse of jargon or technical terms; uses body language, gestures, and eye contact appropriately; uses appropriate visual aids to accompany presentations; able to persuade others to take action; tactful in speaking with others.

Strategic Thinking

Ability to use information about the organization, competition, and market conditions to identify and develop plans to accomplish the goals of the organization.

Able to identify high payoff opportunities and prioritize team efforts in order to better position their organization for future success; looks beyond the current situation based on a broad perspective; effectively balances the need to solve immediate problems while building a system to ensure long-term organizational survival.

Team Building

Ability to help a work group use all of its resources and expertise to manage complex situations and achieve positive results.

Builds an effective team building through attention to how team members relate and how work is accomplished; able to build a cohesive and productive team; instills in team members a sense of pride and satisfaction in the work they accomplish; links people together in such a way that they achieve more than the sum of their individual efforts; creates an environment conducive to team functioning; values the work each member does; encourages interaction among team members; includes team members at all levels in as much decision making, planning, and problem solving as possible; reinforces and recognizes the accomplishment of goals and objectives; discourages isolation of the team from other organizational units and works to increase communication and collaboration across groups.

Versatility

Ability to temporarily modify one's social style in order to meet the needs of others without sacrificing personal integrity.

Able to empathize with others and be helpful without being judgmental; able to deal with difficult people without becoming defensive; accepts others as they are, not as they "should be"; gives people the benefit of the doubt; is attentive and interested in others; treats others with respect; is helpful to others even when they appear to be unappreciative; actively solicits ideas from others who have opposing viewpoints; uses effective listening skills in order to understand another person's point of view; uses strengths to compliment another's weaknesses; works out differences collaboratively and recognizes when compromise is appropriate; understands when it's necessary to "withdraw gracefully" from a disagreement.

Vigilance

Ability to recognize changes in the physical environment in order to alter a course of action or apply corrective measures.

Pays close attention to the physical environment, monitoring for changes which may signal the presence of a problem or the need for action or adjustment; able to handle interruptions without being distracted from completing the task at hand; may use various instruments and tools such as video display terminals, gauges, analog or digital displays, monitors, and the like.

Written Communications

Ability to present ideas and convey information clearly and effectively through formal and informal documents; edits, interprets, and reviews written works by self and others.

Writes at an appropriate level for the intended audience; uses correct grammar, punctuation, and spelling; eliminates unnecessary detail; uses technical terms appropriately; avoids overuse of jargon or technical terms; chooses appropriate charts, graphs and visuals to accompany text materials; clearly and effective communicates ideas or concepts in written form.

Appendix C

Sample Interview Questions

Acumen: Ability to deal effectively with organizational politics and build alliances with people at all organizational levels.

Effectively balances the needs of self and one's own work group with the key objectives, values and mission of the broader organization.

At least once in our working careers we discover that our own goals or the goals of the people we manage are in conflict with the goals of higher management. Tell me about a time when this happened to you.

Able to judge which goals are worth fighting for and when it's best to compromise or "give in."

To be able to judge which goals are worth fighting for and when it's best to compromise or "give in" is a necessary skill for some jobs. Tell me about a time when you felt it was important to either "hold the line" or "give in" to be successful.

Knows the right things to say at the right times.

Being diplomatic in conversations with others is sometimes difficult. Tell me about a time when you found it necessary to be diplomatic when communicating with a person or a group.

Knows when to lead and when to follow.

Tell me about an experience where you had an opportunity to make a choice either to lead or to follow. What choice did you make and how did it turn out?

Effectively uses formal and informal channels to achieve results.

Often it is necessary to use both formal and informal channels of communication in order to achieve a desired result. Tell me about a time when you did this and if it paid off for you.

Adaptability: Ability to demonstrate flexibility in dealing with difficult or unpleasant circumstances, or adjusting to changing conditions, in order to meet job requirements.

Shows resilience in the face of conflict, frustrating circumstances, constraints, rapidly changing circumstances, shifting priorities, adversity, and multiple demands upon time and other resources.

Tell me about a time when rapid change or shifting priorities created a problem for you at work.

Has a high tolerance of ambiguity.

Describe an experience where you had to take action or make a hasty decision without adequate data or information.

Does not become defensive when receiving feedback from others, but instead uses feedback as a tool to do a better job.

Tell me about a time when you received some unpleasant feedback about your work. What did you do?

Works well under stress and pressure.

Give me an example of a time when you had to work under great stress or pressure. Tell me about the situation and what happened.

Able to identify the critical needs in a situation, deal with those, and put the others on the "back burner."

Tell me about a time when you had more problems to deal with than you had time for. How did you handle it?

Analysis: Ability to gather information and extract relevant data and apply it to a current situation in order to arrive at a conclusion, solve a problem, or make a valid decision.

Consults print based or computer based media.

Tell me about an assignment you had which required you to gather a lot of information from printed or computer-based materials.

Uses flowcharts, maps, or network diagrams to help others visualize the interrelationships among data elements.

What experience have you had using flowcharts, maps, or network diagrams to help others visualize the interrelationships among data elements?

Conducts "what-if" analyses to test hypotheses.

Testing hypotheses can be accomplished in several ways such as building models, conducting "what-if" analyses or conducting experiments. Tell me about any experiences you have had in conducting "what-if" analyses.

May use a formal problem-solving method to determine root causes of a problem.

Think of a complex problem you had to solve on your job. Tell me about the process you used to determine the root cause of the problem.

Able to check self and other's logic in order to determine the validity of the conclusion or decision.

A common way to validate a decision or the correctness of a conclusion is to use a process to check your own or another person's' logic. Summarize your experience in doing this.

Assertiveness: Ability to express oneself in a confident manner and maintain a point of view even while experiencing opposition.

Able to achieve the intended result by being persistent without being abusive, violating the rights of others, or verbally attacking another person.

Tell me about a time when you faced resistance or rejection of your ideas or actions. What did you do?

Able to maintain self esteem while being criticized by others; keeps a positive mental attitude which supports the achievement of goals and objectives.

At one time or another, we are the subject of negative criticism by others. Tell me about a time when this happened to you.

Able to say "no" to unreasonable demands of others.

We sometimes run into a person who makes unreasonable demands of us. Tell me about a time when this happened to you.

Questions authority in a tactful way.

Tell me about a time when you felt it was necessary to question or challenge the authority of your boss or upper management. What did you do?

Not threatened by conflict and manages disagreements well.

Highlight your experience in dealing with interpersonal conflict or disagreements by recalling a difficult situation that you were involved in.

Coaching: Ability to evaluate the development needs of employees and provide guidance in improving current job performance or preparing for career advancement.

Able to recognize jobholder's areas of strength as well as areas where development is needed.

Tell me about a situation where you found it necessary to help another person improve their skills.

Encourages jobholder to be proactive in improving their performance or preparing for advancement.

Career development is just one of many management functions. Recall an experience where you worked with one person in this area. What were the person's basic career goals and what did you do to help them prepare for advancement?

Gives employees opportunities to be exposed to other parts of the organization.

Helping employees to grow and develop sometimes means that they must be exposed to other parts of the organization. Give me one example of how you accomplished this in the past.

Monitors day to day work performance and provides regular performance feedback to jobholders.

What have you done in the past, if anything, to monitor the day-to-day work performance and provide regular feedback to the people that you supervised.

Does not punish mistakes, instead, uses them as opportunities for problem solving.

We have a choice to either punish mistakes or use them as an opportunity to help employees develop their skills. Tell me about a time when you chose the option to help an employee improve by avoiding punishment and focusing on problem-solving and development.

Collaboration: Ability to work effectively with others in order to achieve meaningful results.

Displays a willingness to establish alliances and partnerships which may involve the modification of individual needs for the good of the group.

Sometimes we are faced with the choice of standing firm or establishing alliances and partnerships that require us to compromise our own needs for the good of all parties. What have you done when you were faced with a choice like this?

Responds both assertively and cooperatively, actively participating in seeking results which benefit all parties in making plans, solving problems, making decisions, completing tasks, and accomplishing goals.

In our jobs there are times when we have to balance the competing needs of several parties. Tell me about a situation where this happened to you.

Does not use personal or position power to satisfy one's own needs at the expense of others.

Tell me about a time when you chose not to use your personal or position power to satisfy your own needs at the expense of another.

Communicates a willingness to consider the suggestions and ideas of others.

People are often willing to give us ideas and suggestions about how to solve a problem or do our job. Do you usually find these helpful or do they seem to have little value? Give me some details from an experience that represents your position.

Clarifies and communicates agreements, action plans, and goals in order to assure understanding.

Some people believe that to assure understanding and achieve meaningful results it's necessary to clarify and communicates agreements, action plans, and goals. Give me an example from your experience that illustrates your agreement or disagreement with this belief.

Commitment to Quality: Ability to champion the need to deliver quality products and services; to maintain the issue of quality as a primary organizational focus, and to support the concept of "Total Quality Management".

Actively builds strategic alliances with suppliers, vendors, and customers.

What have you done in the past to build strategic alliances with suppliers, vendors, or customers?

Views quality as the responsibility of everyone in the organization.

Many organizations view quality improvement as necessary to their ultimate success. In your experience who is responsible for this in an organization? What have you done to put this belief into action?

Ensures that continuous improvement is in place in all systems and processes.

What have you done to implement continuous improvement in your work group or organization? Is this in place in all systems and processes or in only a selected few?

Works with both internal and external customers to establish quality standards and procedures to measure success.

Summarize your experience in working with both internal and external customers to establish quality standards and procedures. Then, tell me about a situation that was either especially satisfying or frustrating for you.

Fixes quality problems immediately and develops processes or procedures to prevent reoccurrence.

Tell me about an experience where you discovered a quality problem with a product or service. Describe what you did to fix the problem and highlight any processes or procedures you developed to prevent a reoccurrence.

Compliance: Ability to follow established guidelines, policies, and procedures in order to ensure consistency or to protect the safety or preserve the welfare of others.

May use checklists, flowcharts, or decision trees to follow a prescribed sequence.

Detail your experience using tools such as written procedures, checklists, flowcharts, or decision trees in order to follow a prescribed sequence.

Thoroughly and accurately fills out required forms and documents.

Tell me about any jobs or assignments you had that required you to fill out lots of forms or documents.

Able to stick to an established routine over a long period of time.

Certain jobs have established routines that must be faithfully followed. Tell me about a time in your career when you had to stick to an established routine or procedure over a long period of time. How long did this situation last?

Not easily persuaded to make exceptions to policies and guidelines.

Many jobs have established policies and guidelines. Tell me about a time when someone approached you and presented a reason for you to make an exception. What did you do?

Applies policies and regulations consistently to those at all levels within the organization.

Certain jobs require that policies and regulations be applied consistently to people at all levels within an organization Tell me about a time when you felt it was important to do this for consistency, safety or other reasons.

Conflict Management: Ability to work with people at all levels in the organization to create effective solutions and maintain positive working relationships when disagreements arise.

Brings conflict out into the open, does not avoid it or sacrifice own needs in order to placate others.

Sometimes it's necessary to bring conflict out into the open and other times avoid it or sacrifice your own needs in order to placate others. Tell me about a situation where you had to make a choice like this.

Uses facts, not personalities, to reach a decision when an argument develops within the work group.

Sometimes arguments develop between individuals within a work group. Describe a situation where this happened in a work group that you were involved with. What did you do to help resolve the argument?

Uses systematic problem solving techniques to identify the real causes underlying a conflict.

Describe a time when you were able to uncover the real causes underlying a conflict. What exactly did you do?

Uses collaboration whenever possible to build win-win solutions to conflicts.

Tell me about a time when you worked to build a win-win solution to a conflict. This could be a situation where you were in disagreement with another person or where you mediated a dispute between individuals or groups.

Uses mediation or direct confrontation to deal with power struggles and to resolve win-lose situations.

It is sometimes difficult to deal with power struggles or resolve win-lose situations. Tell me about a time when you were successful in such a situation.

Critical Thinking: Ability to examine information, facts and data and make valid judgments based on content and quality.

Makes timely and appropriate decisions under conditions of uncertainty.

Recall a situation where you felt pressured to make a decision even though did not have enough information to be certain of the outcome.

Recognizes when assumptions have been made and whether they are logically valid or invalid based on available evidence.

Tell me about a time when you found it necessary to make assumptions in order to solve a problem, make a decision or cause some action to take place.

Able to determine if arguments are strong or weak.

Tell me about a time when someone presented a weak argument to support their position. How did you determine that the argument was weak? Then tell about a time when someone was able to present a strong argument. How did you determine that this argument was strong?

Able to draw logical conclusions from available information.

Sometimes we lack full information when we are trying to reach a conclusion. Tell me about a time when you were able to draw a logical conclusion from available, but not exhaustive, information.

Weighs the known against the unknown, predicting benefits and costs, and weighing risks.

Making valid judgments requires that we evaluate the content and quality of information. For example, we might weigh the known against the unknown, predict benefits and costs, or evaluate risks, etc. Tell me about a time when you used skills such as these.

Customer Satisfaction: Ability to build productive relationships with internal or external customers in order to build customer loyalty and business success.

Identifies or anticipates customer needs, regularly sets standards that exceed customer specifications, keeps commitments to customers, encourages and uses customer feedback to improve service.

What have you done to ensure that your products or services really meet your customers' needs?

Treats both internal and external customers with the same high level of respect.

Customers can be both external or internal. Tell me about a time when an external customer "tried your patience." Now tell me about a time when an internal customer also "tried your patience."

Trains others in customer service techniques.

Summarize your experience in training others in customer service techniques. Then, tell me about the most challenging situation of this type that you have faced.

Takes responsibility for mistakes in delivery or quality of product or service and atones for the errors.

In spite of our best efforts, sooner or later we all make a mistake in the delivery or quality level of a product or service under our control or influence. Tell me about a time when this happened to you.

Responds in a timely manner to customer phone calls, complaints, and inquiries.

Tell me about a situation where you had to respond to a customer complaint or inquiry. When did you receive the complaint or inquiry and what steps did you take?

Decision Making: Ability to systematically evaluate the positives and negatives of competing choices in order to select the most appropriate alternative.

Able to clearly specify what has to be decided and what result is to be achieved by a decision.

Tell me about a situation that challenged your ability to clearly specify what was to be decided and what result was to be achieved for a decision you had to make.

Able to distinguish between criteria that are desirable, absolutely essential, or unimportant when making a decision.

Tell me about an important decision you made where your ability to distinguish between criteria that are desirable, absolutely essential, or unimportant really paid off for you.

Applies a form of benefit or numerical analysis to evaluate the relative strengths of alternative courses of action when making a decision.

Recall a decision you had to make where there were several possible choices. Tell me about the situation and describe the method you used to evaluate the relative strength of each alternative.

Designs or utilizes tools such as tables, charts, or graphs in order to support a rational decision.

Tell me about your best work in designing or utilizing tools such as tables, charts, or graphs to support an important decision or conclusion you reached.

Weighs the "pros" and "cons" of alternatives to determine which one has the highest payoff for a decision.

Recall a situation where you had to choose one out of several alternatives. Outline the process you used to determine which alternative had the highest payoff.

Decisiveness: Ability to make a decision based on available information and assume the risks involved in order to achieve a desired result.

Able to respond to the imminent need to make a decision and not cause unnecessary delay.

When has a timely decision you made avoided an unnecessary delay in completing a task or achieving an objective?

Not overly influenced by the need to make the "popular" decision.

Tell me about a time when you had to make a decision that you knew would be difficult for others to accept. What happened?

Resists compromise if the desired result will not be achieved.

Tell me about a time when you were proud of your ability to stand firm and resist compromise in order to achieve a desired result.

Knows when it is necessary to make exceptions to the rules or modify established policies and procedures.

Tell me about a time when you made an exception to the rules or modified established policies and procedures. Looking back, was that decision necessary?

Responds effectively to crises or emergency situations.

Tell me about a time when you faced a crisis or emergency situation at work.

Dedication: Ability to fully invest oneself in the job and exhibit a high level of commitment; often makes personal sacrifices in order to get the job done or to handle a temporary increase in the workload.

Able to stick to a task or pursue a goal in the presence of obstacles or other difficulties.

Tell me about a time when your were able to stick to a task or pursue a goal even though it might have been easier not to.

Able to tolerate repetitive tasks over long hours.

Give me an example from your background where you had to do a repetitive task over a long period of time.

Able to maintain enthusiasm in spite of changing priorities, recurring problems, and resource limitations.

Facing changing priorities, recurring problems, and resource limitations often taxes our ability to maintain enthusiasm. Tell me about a time when you had to deal with a situation like this.

Works long hours when necessary.

Tell me about a time when you had to work long hours in order to complete an assignment or accomplish something that was important.

Demonstrates a high level of commitment to the organization through words and actions.

Many organizations value a high level of commitment. Tell me about a time when you demonstrated a high level of commitment to an organization through your words as well as your actions.

Empathic Listening: Ability to listen attentively and to fully and deeply understand a person on an emotional as well as on an intellectual level.

Able to go beyond popular skill based techniques such as "active" or "reflective" listening which focus on the intent to reply, control, or manipulate.

Tell me about a time when you were able to really listen to another person, to fully empathize with them and grasp the emotions behind their message.

Listens not only with the ears but also with eyes and heart.

Tell me about a time when someone who was obviously upset, came to you for guidance in solving a serious problem.

Seeks first and foremost to understand before trying to be understood.

In communicating with others you can either focus on first trying to understand before being understood or vice-versa. Describe an experience that illustrates the sequence you most often use.

Displays a willingness to change an action, opinion, belief, principle, or a value based on what is understood.

Describe a situation where you displayed a willingness to change an action, opinion, belief, principle, or a value based on what you understood that went beyond just the words that you heard.

Avoids giving advice or evaluating the ideas of another person.

When we are listening to another person for true understanding, we can either give advice and evaluate their ideas or avoid doing so. Tell me about a situation that reflects the approach you have most often chosen.

Empowerment: Ability to build a workplace culture in which people take personal responsibility for making themselves and their organization successful.

Actively promotes an "entrepreneurial spirit" within the organization.

What have you done to either promote or discourage an "entrepreneurial spirit" within your work group or your organization?

Gives others the latitude to manage their own responsibilities and the authority necessary to accomplish their objectives.

Tell me about a time when you took a chance by giving another person greater responsibility than you normally would have.

Fosters independent thinking and decision making.

One way to achieve superior results is to encourage independent thinking and decision making in others. Tell me about a time when you were successful in doing this.

Turns people into problem solvers.

Tell me about something that you have done in the past to help someone move from a "complainer" to a "problem solver".

Effectively challenges the bureaucratic status quo and its pressures to be safe, cautious, and compliant.

A popular expression emblematic of bureaucratic organizations is "they don't rock the boat". Tell me about a time you challenged the bureaucratic status quo and its pressures to be safe, cautious, and compliant.

Goal Setting: Ability to set goals for oneself or others that are realistic, time bound, describe the desired result, comprehensive, and stated plainly enough to be understood.

Ensures that individual goals are compatible with organizational goals.

What have you done when there was a conflict between your personal goals and the goals of your organization?

Ensures that goals are realistic and based on available resources and other priorities.

When have you had to set goals that were somewhat less that what you wanted because of limited resources or other priorities?

Describes exactly what result is expected when the goal is achieved.

Describing exactly what result is expected when a goal is achieved is often included as part of the goal setting process. Describe an experience you have had that either confirms or contradicts the value of this idea.

Uses goal-setting as a positive tool for helping oneself and others learn new skills to improve quality and productivity.

Tell me about a time when you found it valuable to use goal-setting as a positive tool for helping yourself or others learn new skills to improve quality and productivity.

Periodically holds progress review sessions to measure progress and modify goals, or to identify or remove barriers to goal attainment.

When working with goals, it is often helpful to periodically review progress toward those goals. Please describe the process you use by giving me an example of a review session you held in the past.

Information Management: Ability to evaluate the requirements of the organization for information and to provide information on a timely basis.

Gives the appropriate people in the organization the information they need when they need it.

Knowing who needs information and when they need it can be of great benefit in achieving results. Describe a situation where you found it necessary to use your skills in this area.

Changes and decisions are communicated in a timely manner.

Recall a situation where you had to communicate an important or unpleasant change or decision to an individual or group.

Gathers data from internal sources such as operating departments and staff organizations.

Providing useful information to others often requires that we gather data from internal sources such as operating departments and staff organizations. Give me an example of a situation that challenged your data gathering ability.

Gathers data from external sources such as government agencies, trade and professional associations, journals, periodicals, newsletters, computerized data bases and systems.

This job requires the ability to gather data from external sources such as government agencies, trade and professional associations, journals, periodicals, newsletters, computerized data bases and systems. Please tell me about the most interesting assignment you have had along these lines.

Utilizes a computerized or manually based management information system to gather, store, and distribute data needed by the organization for planning, control, and decision making.

One important function of information management is to utilize a computerized or manually based management information system to gather, store, and distribute data needed by the organization for planning, control, and decision making. Describe the system you use and then tell me about an incident where you were able to use it to benefit your organization .

Influence: Ability to persuade others to take a course of action or to alter their opinions in the absence of direct authority over them.

Gains support and commitment from others.

Tell me about a time when you really needed an unusual level of support and commitment from someone in your organization in order to accomplish something. What did you do to get it?

Able to present a point of view in a forceful way without offending others.

Describe a situation where you found it necessary to express a point of view that was obviously different from another person or group.

Presents compelling reasons to support proposals and ideas.

We often find it necessary to present compelling reasons to others in order to gain support for our proposals and ideas. Tell me about a time when used this technique to gain a desired result.

Works collaboratively with others to achieve results.

Some people prefer to work alone and others prefer to work collaboratively with others to achieve results. Tell me about a situation that best illustrates your own preference.

Well connected with important people inside or outside the organization.

Tell me about a time when your connections with important people inside or outside your organization played an important part in helping you to achieve your objectives.

Innovation: Ability to generate creative or original solutions to apply to new and existing situations or to tap the creative genius within one's people or customers.

Constantly experiments with new ways to improve on "what is".

There's a saying that goes "If it ain't broke, don't fix it." On the other hand, some people are always experimenting with new ways to improve on "what is". Tell me about an experience that illustrates your attitude about this.

Enjoys playing with ideas and concepts.

Creative people often gain satisfaction by playing with ideas and concepts. Tell me about a time when this was a particularly rewarding activity for you.

Fosters a climate where others feel free to experiment and express ideas without fear of criticism.

Someone once said "You can't learn unless you feel free to experiment and express ideas without fear of criticism." Describe an event from your experience that either supports or challenges this idea.

Challenges those elements of the corporate culture that endorse conformity and compliance and support "the way it has always been done."

You have probably heard people respond to suggestions for change with something like "that's the way it has always been done". Tell me about a time when you challenged those elements of the corporate culture that endorse conformity and compliance.

Permits freedom in allowing others to determine "how to" do things.

One way to tap the creativity of others is to give them freedom to determine "how to" do things. Tell me about a time when this either worked well for you or "backfired."

Integrity: Ability to maintain firm adherence to values and principles even in the face of significant pressure to compromise.

Keeps promises and commitments.

Tell me about a time when you have found it most difficult to keep a promise or commitment to another person or to your organization? What was the final outcome?

Describes things as they really are, does not cover up, falsify information or stretch the truth.

Sometimes people stretch the truth, cover up, or falsify information in order to protect themselves or their organization. Tell me about a time when you either found it necessary to do so or decided not to.

Does not take advantage of another person's weaknesses.

In today's competitive work environment, people's weaknesses sometimes show through. Tell me about a time you detected a weakness in another person. What did you do?

Is fully accountable for words and actions and takes responsibility for mistakes.

Describe a time when you made a mistake and accepted full responsibility for it even though it would have been easy not to.

Demonstrates willingness to make tough decisions.

Tell me about a tough decision you had to make when it would have been easier to compromise.

Leadership: Ability to establish a meaningful vision that defines organizational purpose and through exemplary behavior, expertise, and personal power, directs the thinking and actions of others in order to achieve the desired result.

Stimulates people to stretch and grow, while helping them to overcome obstacles.

Relate an experience you have had in encouraging another person to stretch and grow. What obstacles did they have to overcome and what kind of help, if any, did you give to them?

Helps others to gain confidence and build commitment to the organization's mission.

What have you done to help others gain confidence and build commitment to the mission and goals of an organization of which you were both a part?

Is a model of integrity and hard work — sets high work expectations for self and others.

What have you done in the past that demonstrates a high level of personal integrity. Give me an example of a situation that illustrates your willingness to work hard and do more than is expected of you.

Commands the attention and the respect of people at all organizational levels.

What have you done that illustrates your ability to command the attention and the respect of people at all levels within an organization?

Provides clear direction and sets priorities for the team.

One way we achieve results is to provide clear direction and set priorities for our team. Give me an example of a time when this really paid off for you.

Managing Change: Ability to initiate, implement and promote change in the organization in order to create new business opportunities, meet market demands, develop new technology, respond to customer or employee needs, or maintain continuous improvement efforts.

Anticipates resistance to change and demonstrates a willingness to deal with it as a problem to be solved rather than a personality flaw.

Describe a situation where you had to deal with someone who you felt would be resistant to an impending change.

Creates transition plans to proactively manage change.

Describe a major change that you either brought about or had to manage. Detail the actions you took from start to finish.

Works with other advocates of change in the organization to initiate and support change efforts.

Tell me about a time when you worked with advocates of change in your organization to initiate and support change efforts.

Actively monitors the change process through two-way communication with others.

Tell me about a change process you were involved in and detail the communication process you used to monitor its progress.

Demonstrates support, enthusiasm, and commitment to change.

Change if often difficult to accomplish in an organization. Tell me about a time when you demonstrated support, enthusiasm, and commitment to change in order to overcome resistance and implement an important change.

Managing Diversity: Ability to recognize and effectively employ differences among people in a manner that demonstrates respect for the individual while at the same time achieving the required result.

Through words and actions, fosters appreciation for individual differences regardless of a person's interests, values, lifestyle, race, religion, color, disability, gender, or background.

Tell me about a situation that sums up your experience in dealing with people whose interests, values, lifestyle, race, religion, color, disability, gender, or background are different from yours?

Avoids responding with stereotypical behaviors based on habit, conditioning or socialization.

We sometimes make incorrect assumptions about a person whose background is different from our own. Tell me about an experience where this either created a strained working relationship or a productive one for you.

Views differences among people as an opportunity for learning new approaches to work.

Tell me about an experience where you had an opportunity to work alongside or supervise a person different from you. How helpful were they in giving you an opportunity to learn new approaches to your work.

Confronts racist, sexist and other comments that attack the self-respect of others.

We sometimes hear people make sexist and other comments that attack the self-respect of another person or group. Recall a situation when this happened in your presence.

Builds on the complementary skills of the diverse team in order to utilize the full potential of all employees.

A way to utilize the full potential of all employees is to build on the complementary skills of members of a diverse team. Tell me about a time when you worked as a leader or as part of a diverse team. How did you take advantage of each person's unique skills and background?

Motivation: Ability to create a desire in others to perform at a high level or to modify their attitudes through the use of role modeling, positive reinforcement, and incentives.

Recognizes the achievements of employees in a manner that shows pride in them and demonstrates support.

Give me an example of a time when you took the opportunity to tell your management about the achievements of an employee or co-worker.

Provides opportunities for others to pursue those activities which excite them.

What have you done to enable another person to pursue activities which are motivating and exciting to them?

Looks for opportunities to catch people in the act of doing something right and provides immediate reinforcement.

Some management theorists believe that a manager should look for opportunities to catch people in the act of doing something right and provide them with immediate reinforcement. Tell me about an experience that reflects your position about this belief.

Works at building "spirit" within the work unit.

Give me an example of a time when you decided that your work unit needed some "spirit". Tell me in detail what you did.

Removes barriers within the work system that prevent employees from effectively performing their jobs.

Often there are barriers within our organization that prevent employees from effectively performing their jobs. Recall a time when you helped someone achieve greater results by removing such a barrier.

Organizing: Ability to develop an effective organizational structure, recruit and hire a competent staff, and develop systems, processes, and procedures in order to achieve high quality output.

Analyzes one's organization, looking at reporting relationships and distribution of responsibilities and making changes as necessary.

Tell me about an experience where you made changes in your organization after looking at such things as your mission, goals, reporting relationships and the distribution of responsibilities.

Analyzes work flow and operations performed to eliminate bottlenecks, duplication, and improve efficiency.

Give me an example where you have analyzed work flow or operations performed in order to improve efficiency, eliminate bottlenecks or duplication.

Standardizes work processes using tools such as flowcharts, project planning worksheets and meeting guidelines.

Please detail your experience using tools such as flowcharts, project planning worksheets and meeting guidelines as tools to analyze or standardize work processes.

Examines reward systems, performance planning and review systems, training programs, and information systems to ensure that they support the vision and mission of the organization.

When have you last reviewed the reward systems, performance planning and review systems, training programs, and information systems to ensure that they support the vision and mission of the organization of which you were a part? What changes did you recommend? Which of these were implemented?

Studies other organizations to get ideas on how to improve one's own organization.

There are two places to look for ideas when we have the desire or need to make improvements in one's own organization. We can look inside our own or study another organization. Tell me about a time when you set about to make a significant improvement in your organization. Where did you turn for ideas?

Planning and Scheduling: Ability to develop short and long range plans that are comprehensive, realistic, and effective in achieving established objectives.

Links operational plans to the organization's strategic goals and direction.

Give me an example from your past job experience that high lights your ability to build action plans or create programs that support management's strategic goals and direction.

Determines type and amount of resources necessary to implement a plan.

Determining the type and amount of resources required is often part of the implementation phase for a plan. Tell me about a pro ject you were involved in where you had to do this.

Integrates planning efforts across organizational units

What experience have you had in integrating planning efforts across organizational units? Tell me about a situation that is typical of this kind of activity.

May incorporate formal project management tools such as "Work Breakdown Tables", "Project Master Schedules", "Network Diagrams", and "Responsibility Charts."

Describe an experience using formal project management tools such as "Work Breakdown Tables", "Project Master Schedules", "Network Diagrams", and "Responsibility Charts" as part of your work in planning and scheduling.

Able to troubleshoot plans by identifying potential problems, assessing threat, developing either preventive or contingent actions.

One step in the planning process is to identify potential problems, assess risk, and develop either preventive or contingent actions to deal with these problems. Tell me about a time when this proved to be a worthwhile activity for you or your work team. (Not all elements of a formal plan require this step. Does this person know when to use a formal procedure like this or when a simpler process might be more effective?)

Problem Solving: Ability to systematically organize and evaluate information in order to determine the true cause of a problem and apply corrective action.

Avoids "jumping to solution" until the problem has been clearly defined, relevant facts and data have been gathered, potential causes have been developed, and a most likely cause has been identified.

It's often tempting to immediately "jump to solution" when faced with a problem. Tell me about a time when you resisted this temptation in order to get at the real cause of the problem.

Takes interim actions as necessary to deal with the immediate effects of a problem.

Sometimes a "band aid" is necessary to minimize the immediate effects of a problem before a more permanent fix can be applied. Tell me about a problem you dealt with where such interim actions were required.

Does not take action based solely on "gut feelings" or "best guesses."

In your opinion is it valuable to take action based on "gut feelings" or "best guesses"? Tell me about a situation that supports your perspective.

Looks for the simpler, more practical causes of a problem before testing the more esoteric causes.

When we look for causes of a problem, we either look for uncomplicated causes or more elaborate or unexpected causes. Which of these options has proven to be more effective for you in the past. Illustrate this with an example of an important problem you dealt with.

Uses some type of verification strategy to establish a problem's true cause.

A verification strategy is a useful tool to confirm that you have discovered a problem's true cause. Think of a situation where you used some type of verification technique and discovered that you identified the true cause or discovered that the cause had been misidentified.

Sociability: Ability to approach and interact with others in a warm, friendly, and supportive manner, creating a climate of trust, consideration, and mutual respect.

Responsive to the needs of others for acceptance, warmth, sensitivity or harmony.

Tell me about a time when being responsive or indifferent to the needs of another for acceptance, warmth, sensitivity or harmony paid off for you.

Able to establish rapport even under difficult circumstances.

Tell me about a time when you made a special effort to establish rapport when faced with a difficult or politically sensitive situation.

Enjoys the company of others.

Most people prefer to either work alone or to work with others. Give me an example of a situation that reflects your particular preference.

Proactive in speaking to and maintaining contacts with others.

Tell me about an experience that illustrates your preference to be proactive in speaking to and maintaining contacts with others or to wait for others to speak first or contact you.

Develops an extensive network of contacts.

What have you done to develop your network of contacts. Tell me about one contact that resulted in a relationship that embodies the qualities of trust, consideration and mutual respect.

Spoken Communications: Ability to effectively present ideas, transmit information, or convey concepts to individuals or groups of people of varying educational, cultural, and experience levels.

Able to modify the way one communicates in order to minimize the possibility that the message will be misinterpreted.

Tell me about a specific situation where you found it necessary to modify the way you communicated with another person or group in order to minimize the possibility that your message would be misinterpreted — perhaps a group made up of people of varying educational, cultural or experience levels.

Avoids overuse of jargon or technical terms.

What have you done to ensure that your communication avoids the overuse of jargon or technical terms?

Uses body language, gestures, and eye contact appropriately.

Communication involves not only the spoken word, but also body language, gestures, and eye contact. Tell me about a time when your use of these skills helped you to be a more effective communicator.

Able to persuade others to take action.

Give me an example of a time when you were able to persuade others to act on something that was important to you.

Tactful in speaking with others.

Tell me about a time when you found it necessary to be tactful when speaking to another person or group in order to effectively transmit ideas or convey concepts to them.

Strategic Thinking: Ability to use information about the organization, competition, and market conditions to identify and develop plans to accomplish the goals of the organization.

Able to identify high payoff opportunities and prioritize team efforts in order to better position their organization for future success.

Tell me about a time when you were able to identify high payoff opportunities and prioritize team efforts in order to better position your organization for future success.

Looks beyond the current situation based on a broad perspective.

Tell me about a time when you adopted a long range view that really benefitted you or your organization.

Effectively balances the need to solve immediate problems while building a system to ensure long-term organizational survival.

Give me an example of a time when you had to solve an immediate crisis, while at the same time, continued to do things to insure the survival or your work group or organization in the long run.

Able to identify a competitor's strengths and weaknesses and develop strategies to counteract strengths or gain the advantage by displaying strength in an area where a competitor is weak.

Showcase your ability to identify a competitor's strengths and weaknesses and develop strategies to counteract their strengths.

Able to analyze the potential of an internal or external market and develop plans to position the organization to take advantage of current or future opportunities.

To take advantage of current or future business opportunities, one has to analyze the potential of an internal or external market and develop plans to favorably position the organization. Tell me about any experience you have had in developing this kind of a strategic plan.

Team Building: Ability to help a work group use all of its resources and expertise to manage complex situations and achieve positive results.

Able to create an environment conducive to team functioning.

Describe a situation that illustrates your ability to create an environment that improved the effectiveness of your work team.

Values the work that each member does.

Even though employees differ in their ability, each person makes a unique contribution to the organization. When have you found this to be true of a member of your team, perhaps even for a person who was not usually one of your top performers?

Encourages interaction among team members: includes team members at all levels in as much decision making, planning, and problem solving as possible.

Tell me about something you have done in the past that encourages interaction among your work group members. What have you done to include members of your work team in as much decision making, planning, and problem solving as possible?

Reinforces and recognizes the accomplishment of goals and objectives.

Tell me about something you have you done in the past to reinforce and recognize the accomplishment of your own or another's goals and objectives.

Discourages isolation of the team from other organizational units and works to increase communication and collaboration across groups.

Tell me about a time when you recognized the need to promote increased communication and collaboration between your work team and other organizational units. What caused you to recognize this need and what steps did you take?

Versatility: Ability to temporarily modify one's social style in order to meet the needs of others without sacrificing personal integrity.

Able to empathize with others and be helpful without being judgmental.

Tell me about a situation where you were able to empathize with others and be helpful without being judgmental.

Able to deal with difficult people without becoming defensive.

Describe a situation where you had to deal with a very difficult or disagreeable person. Tell me what you did to handle it.

Accepts others as they are, not as they "should be."

Often we see shortcomings, weaknesses, or faults in others. Tell me about a time when you either accepted somebody as they were or decided it was more important to work with them to correct their faults.

Treats others with respect.

Tell me about a time when you found it necessary to temporarily modify you behavior in order to demonstrate respect for another person.

Is helpful to others even when they appear to be unappreciative.

Some people seem to be unappreciative of things that we do for them. Tell me about a time when you decided to be helpful even though a person or group seemed to be indifferent toward you.

Vigilance: Ability to recognize changes in the physical environment in order to alter a course of action or apply corrective measures.

Pays close attention to the physical environment, monitoring for changes which may signal the presence of a problem or the need for action or adjustment.

What have you done in the past that required you to pay close attention to the environment, monitoring for changes which may signal the presence of a problem or the need for action or adjustment?

Able to handle interruptions without being distracted from completing the task at hand.

Tell me about a time when you were able to remain effective or complete an important task in spite of distractions or interruptions.

May use various instruments and tools such as video display terminals, gauges, analog or digital displays, monitors, and the like.

Tell me about your experience using various instruments and tools such as video display terminals, gauges, analog or digital displays, monitors, and the like in your work.

Able to concentrate for long periods of time on routine work, yet react quickly in an emergency.

A well known quote among pilots is: "Flying is hours of boredom punctuated by moments of stark terror!" What experiences have you had that required you to concentrate for long periods of time on routine work, yet react quickly in an emergency?

Alert to conditions which may cause equipment to malfunction or a process to exceed acceptable control limits.

Tell me about a time when you had to monitor or control the operation of equipment or a process and at the same time be alert to conditions which could cause that equipment to malfunction or the process to exceed acceptable control limits.

Written Communications: Ability to present ideas and convey information clearly and effectively through formal and informal documents; edits, interprets, and reviews written works by self and others.

Writes at an appropriate level for the intended audience.

Give me an example that highlights your ability to modify your writing style in order to reach an audience that functions at a different reading level than your own.

Uses correct grammar, punctuation, and spelling.

Using correct grammar, punctuation, and spelling are requirements for many jobs. Give me an example from your work experience that illustrates the extent of your skills in this area.

Eliminates unnecessary detail in memos, letters, and reports.

Tell me about some writing you have done that illustrates your ability to eliminate unnecessary detail in memos, letters, and reports.

Avoids overuse of jargon or technical terms in written communications.

Sometimes when we write about a subject that is familiar to us we over use technical terms or jargon. Describe a situation where you had to meet such a challenge.

Chooses appropriate charts, graphs and visuals to accompany text materials.

Written material that contains technical, complex or confusing information can sometimes be made more understandable by including appropriate charts, graphs and visuals. Give me an example which illustrates your capability in this area.

Appendix D

Interview Checklist

Interview Checklist

Opening: Set-up/put the Candidate at ease

- ☐ Introduce yourself — smile! Thank the candidate for coming.

- ☐ Offer a refreshment.

- ☐ Review the schedule for the day.

- ☐ Describe the current position and your relationship to the job.

- ☐ Explain the process (Response Pyramid™ and data gathering model).

- ☐ Tell them you will be taking notes and they are free to do so (Comment about confidential information).

- ☐ They may ask additional questions at the end of the interview.

Probing: Learn more about the Candidate

- ☐ Clarify or add information to the resume as needed.

- ☐ Review duties/responsibilities for Candidate's current or last job.

- ☐ Ask pre-written questions, probe for data, and take notes.

☐ Use silence and interruption to maintain control. Seek a balance of information.

Answer questions and sell your organization

☐ Be prepared for questions about benefits, financials, company philosophy, mission, values, job performance criteria, management style, organizational climate, etc.

☐ Sell your organization

Close on a positive note

☐ Explain the next steps in the process.

☐ Thank the Candidate for taking time to come to the interview.

☐ Encourage Candidate to call if they receive offers or have questions.

☐ Give the candidate your business card and other prepared materials.

☐ Escort candidate to the next interview if appropriate.

Index

About Management Development Systems, LLC

Management Development Systems was launched in April, 1986, to help individuals and companies acquire the skills necessary to prosper in an increasingly complex and competitive global business environment.

Our flagship product, *Behavior Based Interviewing (BBI)*, is used by major corporations throughout the U.S. This one-day workshop teaches interviewers how to effectively apply the information and techniques discussed in *High Impact Hiring*.

We also make available a series of one-day and half-day legal workshops to help companies prevent employee lawsuits. *Managing Within the Law* workshops are led by experienced attorneys who strip away "legalese" and make the law easy to understand.

Contact us at 1-800-353-1669 for more information or to schedule workshops for your organization.

Visit our web site at http://www.hireup.com

Order Form

Telephone Orders: Call Toll Free (800) 353-1669.

Internet Orders: Visit our web site at http://www.hireup.com

Mail Orders: Management Development Systems, LLC
32352 Ascension Road, Dana Point, CA 92629-3602.

Description	Qty	Price Each	Amount
📖 *High Impact Hiring*		$ 29.95	
Video — How to Interview and Hire The Best		$ 99.00	

Sub-total this order: _____

Sales Tax (for CA residents, add 7.5%): _____

Shipping: ($4.95 first item, $3.00 each additional item): _____

Total amount of this order: _____

Enclose check or money order for total amount of order and mail to Management Development Systems, LLC 32352 Ascension Road, Dana Point, CA 92629-3602.

Name:_____

Address:_____

City:_____

State:_____ Zip code:_____

Telephone Number:_____